take the
# ride
OF
your life!

**What readers and audiences
alike are saying about ...**

# Take the Ride of Your Life!

*The idea of looking back to your first bike lesson to find
your essential strength in life is a tremendous concept. And
it works! By helping me remember and bring my bike story
to life in this book, Joyce helped me recognize new sources
of energy and vitality in myself and to keep this process
going. This is essential to me as an artist.*

– Monte Nagler, fine arts photographer,
student of the late Ansel Adams, and
author of *How to Improve Your Photographic
Vision* and *Statements of Light*

*Joyce Weiss has an amazing ability to help people see
how simple it can be to "shift gears," to make those small
changes that can lead to such dramatic and overwhelm-
ingly positive improvements, both at work and in their
personal lives.*

– Bob Danzig, author, speaker, professor, and
former Nationwide CEO of Hearst Newspapers

*When Joyce Weiss speaks to our employees, the ratings
are off the chart! She absolutely has what it takes to help
our people go for their full potential and then translate that
into greater productivity and passion for everything they do.*

– Laura Good, Human Resource & Training
Specialist, PARDA Federal Credit Union

*This book is clear, organized, and logically sequential. The examples are helpful in applying the content and concepts to life's situations. Well-written and applicable to readers of all ages and walks of life.*

– Virginia Hosbach, Coordinator, Dept. of Health Care
Education, Blue Cross/Blue Shield of Michigan

*I've never seen so many good and useful ideas between the two covers of a book. Bravo, Joyce. You've done it again. This latest book is pure genius!*

Mark "Doc" Andrews, Sports Director,
CBS-FM Radio, Detroit

*Terrific stuff, Joyce! You're an endless source of practical ideas and great inspiration for getting everyone involved in turning around potentially negative situations. The bicycle analogy is something we can all relate to and is a truly inspirational message.*

– Bill Zehnder, President, Bavarian Inn
Restaurant, Frankenmuth, Michigan

*An entertaining, fun-filled book with inspirational, common-sense ideas guaranteed to motivate its reader. Joyce Weiss knows her stuff.*

– Robert L. Shook,
New York Times best-selling author

# take the ride
## OF
## your life!

Shift Gears for More
Balance, Growth and Joy

## Joyce Weiss

Bloomfield Press ✦ Michigan

*Take the Ride of Your Life* © 2002 by Joyce Weiss

Bloomfield Press
P.O. Box 250163
West Bloomfield, MI  48325-0163

Illustrations by Steve Ferchaud
Interior design by Sara Patton
Printed in the USA

ISBN 09648560-0-X
Library of Congress Catalog Card #2001093628

# Contents

# Dedication

This book is dedicated to my parents, Sara and Joseph Morris. Thanks for giving me the love, values, and skills necessary to take the ride of my life. These gifts have encouraged me to help others achieve their own balance and joy.

# Acknowledgments

I want to send a huge thank you to:

Jerry, my wonderful husband. You are the best. You cheered me at every victory and supported me during the challenges.

My children, Ron, Wendy, Jodi, and Brian, who endured countless hours of listening to me talk about the latest concepts. I really appreciate your endless patience.

My grandchildren, Jordyn, Justin, and Dylan, for helping me see life through your gleeful eyes.

Marcia Miller, my sister, who has always been my personal coach. I'm grateful for your straightforward input and editing, and for believing in what I do professionally and personally.

Robert Weiss, my attorney, whose expertise helped me with all the legal ramifications of writing and publishing this book.

David and Lisa Sawicki, for your insights, support, and excitement about this book. You even wrote a song especially for *Take the Ride of Your Life!* Your talent and friendship mean so much to me.

Sandy Bradshaw, the first person who started on this journey with me. I value the time you took for taping interviews and bringing the stories to life.

Susan Suffes, editor extraordinaire, who took the manuscript to the next level. Going way beyond my expectations, you took the stories and blended them naturally with the chapters.

Humorist David Glickman, who created such a terrific subtitle and catchy chapter titles. Your talents gave the book an element of fun. I'm delighted that you shared my vision and passion.

Pam Lontos, Quetsy Pucket, and everyone at PR/PR Public Relations, my talented PR colleagues, for your help and unstoppable efforts in marketing *Take the Ride of Your Life!* Your energy and enthusiastic nature mean so much to me.

Del Reddy, Vice President of Power Play International, Inc., who works with Gordie and Colleen Howe, for being so helpful in attaining some incredible testimonials.

Sam Horn, for writing the brilliant chapter titles. Your talents beamed every time we spoke.

My publisher, Nikki Stahl from The Jenkins Group, for your patience and willingness to honor my message. I changed directions many times and you never complained.

Graphic artist Kathi Dunn, for your brilliant talent in designing the perfect cover for the book.

Susan Kendrick, for writing such a catchy back cover and for making the book easy and exciting to read. I appreciate your tremendous talent and professionalism.

Melanie Swords-Beverly, for your valuable editing and typing contribution.

Sara Patton, for editing the manuscript toward the end of the project and for typesetting — making the inside of the book as beautiful as the outside.

Steve Ferchaud, for designing the art illustrations for each chapter and the book cover. You added such an element of fun to the book.

Tami DePalma from Marketability Book Publicity and Promotion, for designing the smashing marketing plan for *Take the Ride of Your Life!*

Julie and Nick Hunkar from JH Webworks, for introducing this project to the Internet. People are now ordering products and services worldwide because of the masterful web site you created.

All the people whose experiences, both joyful and painful, are included here. Your stories, so honest and authentic, are an inspiration. Others will gain such value from your personal histories.

My clients, loyal friends, and colleagues from the National Speakers Association, who kept on asking me when this book would be done. I value your enthusiastic interest and helping to make my career worthwhile and positive.

It's a delight knowing all of you. I feel privileged that together we have been able to create *Take the Ride of Your Life!*

# take the
# ride
## OF
## your life!

# Introduction

When people ask me how I got the idea for *Take the Ride of Your Life!*, I tell them that the inspiration was simple.

A few years ago, I went to Dallas to meet with Juanell Teague, a professional speaker's coach. She gave me an assignment before my session with her: Make a list of the turning points in my life and figure out how they have impacted who I am today.

One turning point I identified was a lesson I learned when my father taught me how to ride my two-wheel bike—without the training wheels.

I remember the day I got that bike. It was red with white streamers flowing from the handlebars. I was so excited; I was also scared out of my mind. You see, I wasn't as physically coordinated as some of my friends. I was always—I mean *always*—the last one chosen for kickball.

Fortunately, my father understood me. He knew how embarrassed I would be trying to learn to ride my bike with all my friends watching from their front porches on Kentucky Street in Detroit. He wanted to take me to a place where I would be comfortable. So, every night after he came home from work, we would walk my new bike to the empty parking lot next to the bank. There were no cars or people in sight.

Then he would give me a pep talk: "Falling is okay. I know you will eventually learn if you trust yourself. Are you ready? Get on that bike. Pedal . . . pedal . . . pedal." Inspired, I eagerly hopped on the bike and, just as quickly, fell off.

My dad told me, "Remember, I said you might fall. It's okay. Just get back on." I got back on and fell again.

"Remember, I said to trust yourself, honey?" my father coaxed. "Practice makes perfect!" Determined, I got back on. And I fell once more—and not for the last time.

Still, my father was right. I finally did learn to ride my bike. He knew I could do it. Through all my spills, I always heard his message: "Trust yourself. It's okay to fall. Just get back on and pedal. Practice makes perfect."

Juanell immediately responded to my story and suggested that it was deeply related to who I am today. I started sharing my bike story with my audiences. They connected with me like never before in my fifteen years as a professional speaker! Many thanked me because my insights gave them the hope that they could find their own "bike stories" to help them move ahead.

Audience members immediately started telling me their most cherished childhood memories of their bikes. I heard vivid tales about long-ago Schwinn Phantoms, Roadmasters, Huffys, and Evans Colsons. Others remembered muscle bikes, Stingrays, ten speeds, mountain bikes, and the tat-a-tat sound of playing cards flapping in the spokes. Banana seats, high-rise handlebars, and fenders were all fondly remembered.

Soon the "bike stories" themselves started rising to the surface. I discovered that many people, like me, gained their first real sense of self-reliance and responsibility while learning to ride a bike.

"Who taught you?" "What lessons did you learn?" and "What about you is the same now as when you were a little girl or boy?" became part of these conversations. The deeply personal impact of each person's bike-riding lesson was so interesting and enlightening, these stories naturally became a rich and exciting part of this book.

You'll hear stories from people who share their own "Ride of Your Life" experiences — the dreams, the growing pains, the triumphs, the many falls, and what made them get up and try again.

The subject of each chapter came from the themes and patterns that emerged in these interviews. At the end of each chapter I have included exercises, which I call Gear-Shifting Action Steps, that helped me when I was on my discovery journey with Juanell. I hope you will be inspired to use them, too.

Do you remember pedaling your bike up a hill? You reached the top and then started down, faster and faster. The wind blew in your face as trees, houses, and cars whizzed by. It was an unforgettable ride.

Come take that "ride" again. This book gives you the tools and inspiration you need to climb the hills, maneuver the twists and turns, and experience the thrill of your own journey—no matter where your ride in life may take you.

## A Brief History of the Bicycle

The journey of writing this book took my husband and me to the most charming and interesting place, the Bicycle Museum of America in New Bremen, Ohio. Founded by Jim Dicke in 1997, the museum houses one of the leading collections of antique and classic bicycles in the United States. The museum has been very gracious in allowing me to use its information, photographs, and cartoons.

At the museum we learned that Baron Von Drais, a landscape gardener, designed one of the first functioning two-wheelers, the Draisine, in Germany. The Draisine had no pedals; riders used their feet to propel the bike. It was just a little faster than walking.

By 1898, women were riding adult tricycles. American feminist leader Susan B. Anthony said, "Let me tell you what I think of bicycling. I think it has done more to emancipate women than anything else has in the world. I stand and rejoice every time I see a woman ride by on wheels. It gives a woman a feeling of freedom and self-reliance."

Orville and Wilbur Wright created a lucrative business repairing and building bicycles. Their lightweight airplane was built like a bike. Spoke wires stabilized the wings and chains drove the dual propellers.

By 1934, Frank Schwinn, an engineer whose family company had been making bikes since 1895, designed the first balloon tire for a bicycle and added big fenders and headlights. He realized that kids wanted their "wheels" to include automobile features.

Sadly, the Depression forced many bicycle companies out of business. Undeterred, Schwinn built the Aerocycle and painted it silver, just like an airplane.

By 1947, Schwinn, Shelby, Rollfast, and Roadmaster expanded the bicycle industry and added accessories like headlights, reflectors, horns, and new suspension systems. The Black Phantom was the biggest post-war winner in 1949. With all its shiny chrome, the model became the hit of the playground.

Kids liked the Hopalong Cassidy and the Donald Duck models in the 1950s. Stingrays, Krates, and Mongooses became bestsellers in the 1960s. Today Gen-Xers enjoy free-styling on mountain bikes and BMX classics. There is even an electric model called the E-bike. Lee Iacocca designed it in 1999. Even today, we have an endless fascination with the bicycle as an enduring symbol of perfect freedom and adventure on a truly human scale.

# chapter 1

# Stress

## "I'm Afraid to Take Off the Training Wheels!"

## Go From Fear to In-Gear

Long ago in a faraway land, brutal warlords ravaged the countryside. They took over the villages, ruining the lives of the farmers who lived there. There was one farmer who still had some land. He also had a son and he owned a horse.

Every evening the neighbors gathered to console each other. They looked at the farmer with envy and said, "You have such good luck. Everything good happens to you." The farmer simply shrugged his shoulders, and said, "Good luck, bad luck, who knows?"

One day the farmer's horse ran off and disappeared. That same day, the warlords rode into the village and killed all the other farmers' horses. The neighbors looked at the farmer and said, "You have such good luck." The farmer replied, "Good luck, bad luck, who knows?"

A few days later the farmer's horse returned. His son was happy to see the horse. He jumped up on the horse's back and galloped off for a ride. Suddenly, the horse tripped over a rock. The son fell off the horse and broke his leg.

The warlords soon returned and demanded the villagers' able-bodied sons for a battle. As the sons were marched away, the villagers looked at the farmer and said, "You have such good luck.

Your son was of no use to the warriors with his broken leg." The farmer shrugged his shoulders and said, "Good luck, bad luck, who knows?"

## The Power of "Pedal On"

You can either be like the farmer or his neighbors. The farmer realizes that things happen in life. We can't label them good or bad right away. We have to give life a chance. The neighbors, on the other hand, are too ready to take on the role of victim. No matter what happens, they feel they are on the losing end of any situation and that there is nothing they can do about it. They don't know how to "look" for other perspectives, other ways of seeing and living.

We can accept the things that happen to us without labeling them good or bad, lucky or unlucky. Losing a job, for example, may seem bad at the time. New and exciting opportunities, however, can arise from this circumstance. It can turn out for the best—if you maintain a positive attitude. It's not what happens that shapes us; it's how we react to it.

Do you have a PO approach to life? I'm not just talking about attitude or a positive outlook, but rather an action, the courage to "pedal on" when stressful things happen. In bicycle terms, it means taking off the training wheels and facing your fear. It's what helps you really get rolling whether you think you're ready or not.

When I hear somebody sigh, "Life is hard," I am always tempted to ask, "Compared to what?" Human experience would lose something very important if there were no roadblocks to

> *Life is a grindstone, and whether it grinds you down or polishes you up is for you alone to decide.*
>
> – Cavett Robert, founder of the National Speaker's Association

overcome. The journey would not be half so wonderful if there were no steep hills to climb or the thrill of the wind in your face as you cruise down the other side.

Still, it is tough to stay upbeat in these chaotic times. That's why "pedaling on" is a necessary survival skill.

I discovered the true power and scope of a positive outlook when I met Joe, the tire changer at a local service station. He gave me a huge grin when I told him I needed my tires checked. Immediately Joe turned on his radio, started his timer, and began his routine. He sang, smiled, and swayed with the music during the entire operation. The moment he was done, he turned off the timer. "I did it! I broke my record!" he yelled so that everyone in the garage could hear him. "I knew I could do this!" he exclaimed.

How often do we dread the routine parts of our jobs? Many of us have days that seem like the same old thing over and over. I don't think Joe ever experienced days like that. He took his job seriously, but with a flair and attitude that made it challenging and fun. Joe's manager told me that the morale of the shop had skyrocketed since he hired Joe. The other employees enjoyed being around him and encouraged him to break more records. They have also taken on some of his positive spirit in their own jobs.

## Stories of Triumph — "What's in a Bike?"

**SVETLANA**

Svetlana, a nail technician, is a woman who refused to let her sad Russian childhood get in the way of her future happiness. Growing up in a tiny apartment with her younger sister and mother, Svetlana took care of the house while her mother worked. Her father was away most of the time in the military.

The pivotal event of teaching Svetlana how to ride a bike, therefore, fell to the neighbors. Suddenly Svetlana found an escape. The first time she learned to balance and took off down a frozen Moscow street, she felt the exhilaration of freedom.

Today, in the United States, Svetlana and her husband nurture and cherish their son, teaching him to be open, honest, and loving.

## JOAN

Joan, an entrepreneur, is another courageous woman who has both fond and painful memories of growing up. On the one hand, she adored the friendly Detroit neighborhood where children ran in and out of each other's homes, and mothers were always handing out cookies. On the other hand, she was stifled by the atmosphere in her own home, where "children should be seen and not heard" was her parents' motto.

Over time, Joan learned about herself, and in doing so bolstered her weakened self-esteem. "Once I understood where I was coming from and got to know myself, I realized I was okay," she said. "Acknowledging my positive attributes—my sense of humor, loyalty, perseverance, honesty, and the ability to have fun—led me to accomplish a lot as a parent and a wife, and with my work. I realized the security of home is very important. To me, a bike represents taking off to somewhere new and unknown."

## DAVID

David, an accountant, related this story: "As a boy, I knew my father was proud of me. Unfortunately, he didn't know how to show it. There wasn't a whole lot of positive attitude in my house," David remembered. The dictum, "You must behave," was drilled into him and his siblings time and time again.

"In school I was the class clown. I couldn't talk at home," he said, "so I had to express myself elsewhere."

David was around ten or eleven years old when he learned how to ride a bike. "Some friends taught me. I used a neighborhood boy's bike; I didn't have one of my own. I fell down, and got up again right away. I felt good whenever I was on a bike, as if anything was possible."

David's wife has helped him focus on keeping a positive attitude.

> *You can't be brave if you've only had wonderful things happen to you. As I look back on the times in my life that taught me the most, they were the difficult times. By surviving them, I gained a confidence in myself I never could have achieved if I'd led a totally happy life.*
>
> – Mary Tyler Moore, actress

Before they were married she told him: "I won't marry you if you become like your father." Today, David is grateful. "I don't want to raise my kids the way my father raised me."

## TOM

Tom, a successful salesperson, was told at an early age not to believe in himself. "You are a loser. You will never amount to anything. You will never learn to ride your bike, either," his father said. Those cruel words pounded into Tom's subconscious and took root.

Despite the expectation of failure and the utter lack of love and support, Tom was determined to learn.

As an adult, he became obsessed with success at work. "I cannot fail!" he would tell himself. This became the entire focus of his life, affecting his family and even his health. Rather than relishing his success, he was afraid of "falling off the bike" of his youth. He did not realize he was a winner from the first time he "pedaled" with determination to succeed on his own.

Eventually, Tom was able to see all the positives in his life and discovered that he trusted himself all along. He realized he was not only strong and determined—he was a success!

## MONICA

Monica, a freelance web designer, has an incredibly positive outlook today, especially as a woman who overcame depression.

She tells of her first bike, a blue one. Her dad taught her how to ride and she learned very fast. "Dad was always very cautious, whether it was when I learned to ride a bike or when I started to date." When she learned how to ride a bike it helped her gain more independence. "I remember riding farther and farther away, toward more forbidden places."

As a parent, she enjoyed teaching her sons to ride their bikes. "My older boy, who is now eleven, learned to balance on his bike when we removed the pedals. He would get up really early and practice before school. Once he found his balance, we reattached the pedals. Now he's off exploring with his friends and even going off-road.

"Sure, he's had some bad falls. But what is so fascinating is that before he learned to ride, he was very cautious. The occasional scrape would reduce him to tears. Now, he races up to the house, hops off the bike, puts on a Band-Aid, and he's gone again. He's become so much braver—and tougher—since he got his 'wheels.' Our younger son is now on his way to learning to manage a two-wheeler. My husband went out and bought us all bikes so that we can ride together as a family."

Consider the following quote: "I have missed more than 9,000 shots in my career. I have lost almost 300 games. On twenty-six occasions I have been entrusted to take the game winning shot . . . and missed. I have failed over and over and over again in my life. And that is precisely . . . why I succeed."

Do you know who said this? It was Michael Jordan, one the most accomplished sports legends of all time.

We think of poets, artists, and dancers as the passionate people in our society. They ooze enthusiasm and passion for what they do. But you don't need to write, paint, or dance to experience such fulfillment. The challenge is to look at your job and your life, no matter how stressful they might be, and discover how to put that sense of newness and excitement back into the routine, just like Joe the tire-changer did. What can you do to put more thrill and adventure back into your life?

## Overcoming the Negative

For every Joe or Michael Jordan, there are at least ten gloomy pessimists and cynics out there. Cynicism is a cover-up for pain; pessimism is a protection from disappointment. Both are expressions of anger and hopelessness. People who exhibit these traits are frustrated. They feel disappointment in others, and in life itself. It is essential to train ourselves to be optimistic—especially with so many potentially negative people and conditions all around us.

Pessimists in my audience tell me that corporate speakers don't really know what goes on at their workplace. They say things like, "The motivational speaker will waste our time with optimistic fluff," or "This information does not fit in here. Things will not change because of what our managers are doing." They roll their eyes and make sarcastic comments when speakers talk about making positive changes.

I counter with straight talk. Immediately I confront these cynics by saying, "I know there may be some people in the audience who are not as hopeful or full of optimism as others are in this room.

"Can you see how negativity may be blocking your view of opportunities that may exist right here, right in front of you, right now? Look closely. Are there any ways in which your own negativity is shutting out the potentially life-changing views of those around you? Are the roadblocks in your path there because you put them there or allowed someone else to? The good news is that your ride through life depends on choices, and most of these choices are yours to make."

I then ask for volunteers to share how they changed from being negative to being more open to the views of others.

I challenge every person in my audience to ask themselves if they are coaches helping the company grow, or negative road-blocks stopping any progress. The choice is always there.

There will always be cranky people who refuse to hear any positive message. Don't get me wrong; we need to hear complaints and other points of view. This is how we find out what needs to be improved. The challenge is to make sure our criticism is viewed as constructive—not destructive. Any of us can plant the seed; it is up to each one of us to grow with the message.

A friend once confided to me that the moment she graduated from college, her aunt began giving her negative messages. "You have just lived the best years of your life," she kept saying. "You will now enter the cold, hard, real world where you'll have to pay your dues and claw your way to the top."

We tend to take advice like this as if it were the truth. Instead, we need to listen carefully to the message, consider the source, and decide whether or not we *choose* to make it part of our truth. If the message clouds your dreams, you need to get rid of it—and the messenger—immediately. You have the ability to create your own life through choices and decisions that are best for *you*.

## PHOEBE

Phoebe, a paraprofessional, learned early how to overcome cynical people. Her memory of the honeysuckle-perfumed air of North Carolina is one of the best of her complicated childhood. Raised by a controlling mother and stepfather, she cherished the times spent with her beloved great-grandmother.

Phoebe clearly remembers learning to ride a bicycle. "My impatient stepfather asked one question over and over again: 'Why can't you learn to ride?' " she recalls. "And I did have trouble doing it. I knocked out my two front teeth falling off that bike. Another time, my ankle caught in the spokes. I was so badly injured that I required a skin graft."

Walking with a limp for the rest of her life was a possibility because Phoebe refused to put weight on the hurt ankle. And only by putting stress on it could it become strong again.

"One day I found a ring in a store and asked my mother if I could have it. When she said 'no,' I stomped my injured foot. My limp disappeared. While I didn't get the ring, I did get back on my bike."

She understands her bike story was a learning experience, but not one to be repeated by her daughter. "When she fell off her bike with the training wheels on, I told her she would fall down a lot more when they came off. That's what happens when you learn something new. My advice was simple: Wear long pants, and get back on the bike."

## NATALIE

Natalie, a production manager for a publisher, also learned to channel the stresses of childhood into adult strengths. She used her bicycle to escape her critical dad and alcoholic mom.

"My father taught my brothers and me to ride bicycles. He was a schoolteacher and had patience with everyone but his own children. He tried using anger to motivate me. He'd say, 'Come on, you can do this. Don't be a wimp.' Being told this in earshot of the neighborhood kids was mortifying.

"Once I learned how to ride, I would get on my bike and go wherever the bike would take me. Sometimes it would be to a friend's house, sometimes a ride around the city. I would pedal along highways and even on unpaved, bumpy roads. When things were really bad at home, I would head miles north to get to a beach. My head always felt clearer there. I would often daydream about what life could be like as I rode."

Self-motivated and self-sustaining, Natalie took the negative lessons of her parents and turned them into positives for herself and her daughter. She learned courage on her bike.

## Develop Optimism, Enhance Your Life

Explore a couple of ways to develop optimism, the ultimate survival skill.

First, protect yourself from others who try to infect you with their anger. Numerous people have told me they leave the room when someone tries to pull them down. This sends a strong signal to the "downer" that others are unwilling to participate in negative attitudes. This is a very healthy protective skill. This skill is so essential, I have another suggestion from my first book, *Full Speed Ahead: Become Driven by Change*—"Don't walk away from negative people—Run!"

We react in several different ways when others say things that push our buttons. Sometimes we defend ourselves; other times we say nothing. How often have you thought of the perfect response later in the day? There may have been occasions when you said something and wished you had kept your mouth closed. Rather than pushing back, getting even, or suffering in silence, you can gain control and deal diplomatically with unkind people and behavior.

The way to do this—diffuse pessimism and create optimism— is called "verbal aikido." Aikido is a Japanese form of self-defense employing holds and principles of non-resistance to debilitate the strength of an opponent. The aikido practitioner seeks to counter an attack without bringing harm to the attacker in order to create balance and restore harmony to the relationship. In other words, when pushed, pull; when pulled, push.

This technique is just as effective with verbal attacks. It teaches how to respond to an attack. Accepting, redirecting, and

> *No pessimist ever discovered the secret of the stars, or sailed to an uncharted land, or opened a new doorway for the human spirit.*
> – Helen Keller, author

> *An optimist sees an opportunity in every calamity;*
> *a pessimist sees a calamity in every opportunity.*
>
> – Sir Winston Churchill

reaffirming are the tools. This process helps us remain positive and not defensive. It also helps us avoid emotional obstacles without hostility toward the other person.

The cardinal rule of verbal aikido is to not repeat the accusation. For instance, if someone asks, "Why are you wasting my money?" don't say, "We're not wasting your money." Instead, respond with, "Let me tell you what we are doing with your money." This response gives the person nothing to push against. Another example might be, "You're too emotional and you yell too much!" React by pulling away and saying, "I agree with you. I do overreact. It must be frustrating for you." This response diffuses the confrontation and works toward repairing the situation. Verbal aikido is a skill that gives you back the control. It helps you focus on what can be done, versus playing the "blame game."

Here are some other powerful tips to disarm toxic comments.

1.  Ask yourself, "How would I feel if I were in that person's shoes?" Try to figure out why the person is behaving this way. Doing so will help you respond, not react. For example, every time I see a rude customer service representative, I actually do my best to find out the other side of the story. Why is she like this? Could it be the boss just ridiculed her in front of customers? Did someone insult her? Is she thinking of her child's gymnastic class or ball game that she must miss because the company is short-staffed? This is another way to gain control and not sweat the small stuff. (This may also help you to stay calm when you encounter a sarcastic worker.)

One of my clients was very cynical. He saw projects and meetings as a pain in the neck and a hassle. He used to drive me up the wall with his negative comments and lack of enthusiasm. I decided to "walk in his shoes" to get a feel for both sides of the situation. I discovered he was taking an anti-depressant medication. Once I understood this, our conversations became easier. I knew I had to present my ideas differently. I communicated using words that were more appropriate for his personality, and our meetings became more enjoyable for both of us.

2. Don't explain or defend yourself when something goes wrong. Be accountable! Explanations come across as excuses. Agree, if what is being said is true. Acknowledge, apologize, and act. For example, if a customer yells at you for not receiving an item he requested two weeks ago, don't blame it on someone else, even when you know who made the mistake. Try, "You're right, it has been two weeks. I apologize for this and will get it to you today. Please call me tomorrow if you don't receive it."

This technique helps you roll with the punches; it gives you prepared flexibility. Remember, how you react to a negative situation is more important than your actual stress level.

Life is like a grapefruit. First, you pierce through the skin and take a couple of bites to get used to the taste. Just as you begin to enjoy it, you get a squirt in the eye. Nonetheless, the grapefruit is worth the bother. Likewise, a change in behavior is at first uncomfortable, but well worth the effort.

## Letting Go

We all know we are supposed to accept the things we can, and let go of the things we can't. This is a basic yet difficult concept. We waste too much time agonizing over things beyond our control. It is much healthier to turn our attention to what we can control in order to change and improve those situations.

> *I've had a lot of trouble in my life, most of which never happened.*
> – Mark Twain, author

> **The reasonable man adapts himself to the world; the unreasonable one persists in trying to adapt the world to himself.**
>
> – George Bernard Shaw, playwright

My husband Jerry and I recently went on a bus tour through Spain. Our luggage didn't make it from Amsterdam to Madrid. People on our tour were amazed at how well we managed without our bags. I kept telling them we didn't want to put a damper on a dream vacation. And guess what? Our clothes finally arrived. Life goes on despite inconveniences. It's much more important to put energy into controllable situations than to complain about the uncontrollable ones.

There is nothing we have less control over than the past. When a daughter says, "I had too much fun in college, and my resume doesn't look as good as I wish it did," she is admitting her mistake. She realizes her behavior was not the wisest. She has accepted responsibility and is ready to make changes. This is not the time to say, "I told you that you should have studied." We don't need to punish ourselves or others so much. We need to concentrate on the future and let mistakes energize, not immobilize, us. Remember, when the going gets tough, the tough start pedaling.

Letting go is a powerful stress reliever. Ask yourself how important a stressful situation will be two years from now. Deal with it, if it will make an impact on your life. If not, do your best to release the worry and accept the situation for what it is.

## Accepting Others

While verbal aikido can help us control our responses to others, we have no control over others or their responses toward us. We are not all the same; we don't all look or think the same.

When we don't understand this, we try to change everyone to look and act like us. We try to control their existence. Not only is this very dangerous, it is impossible, and therefore it creates a negative atmosphere.

A large part of acceptance is the gift of being non-judgmental. When we are truly interested in people and do not judge them, we feel less frustration with others and therefore place less stress on ourselves.

On a personal level, some relationships can be difficult. Wanting to be accepted when we enter relationships is a given. However, we must also be prepared for rejection and not take it personally. I know there will be trouble the moment I hear someone talk about how he or she wants to change someone else. It helps to realize instead that it is often we who must change in order to more fully accept others. This attitude paves a much smoother road for any relationship.

There was a woman who carried unresolved issues from a breakup with an old boyfriend for years. When she finally had the chance to hear his reason for ending the relationship, he said, "You are too strong for me." She then asked her husband what had attracted him to her. "I love your deep strength and intensity," he said. "We can always agree to disagree."

From Izzy Gesell, a friend and improvisational expert, I learned an exercise that helps us deal with this kind of situation. It is called "Yes, and . . ." Two people have a conversation by starting each sentence with "Yes, and . . ." instead of "Yes, but . . ." This allows each person to accept the other person's words, even though he may not agree with them.

> *In the face of an obstacle which is impossible to overcome, stubbornness is stupid.*
>
> – Simone de Beauvoir, writer and feminist

## Problem-Solving

Life means getting into or out of a crisis most of the time. Instead of lying in bed feeling angry, hurt, or worried, take the stress associated with crisis and turn it into positive energy. Figure out what you need to do to create a more fulfilled life. Problem-solve, be innovative, and don't be afraid to ask for help!

**ALYCE**

Alyce is a crisis counselor for abused women. She understands the power of asking for and giving help.

She spent her earliest childhood in a Louisiana migrant camp. She remembers watching her mom pick tomatoes, cucumbers, strawberries, apples, peaches, and cherries under broiling southern skies.

"My first bike did not even have wheels. It was a real old Schwinn. Everybody took turns pushing each other on it, because it didn't pedal," she recalled.

"It had a big seat on it, and we pretty much taught ourselves to 'ride' it. All the kids took turns holding the bike and pushed each other until we skinned our knees. We had a ball."

It wasn't until Alyce turned eleven or twelve and moved to Michigan that she got her first new bicycle. The family experienced racism in their new neighborhood, but young Alyce and her sisters bounced right through it. "We were the first black people to move in. For a long time, the other parents wouldn't let us play with their children," she says. "Eventually the kids outgrew it; we didn't scare easily and we didn't know any better. We'd still go over to play even if they yelled at us."

Despite the pain racism caused, Alyce's mother never allowed her daughters to behave that way in return. "The prejudice made me a stronger person. It made me realize that no matter what color a person is, you treat them the way you want to be treated."

Today Alyce's home has become a shelter for the homeless. "I always have a house full of children," she says matter-of-factly.

> **Different equals different. Different does not equal wrong.**
> — Joyce Weiss

"They're people; something I do or say may help them. Why should I be the one to turn them away? I want everyone to remember and say, 'She helped me.' "

When Alyce thinks about her bikes she has some keen insights. "That first bike wasn't complete. Yet, a bunch of kids got together and supported each other so we could all play. Then all of a sudden, I had a bike that I could ride myself. It's like my life. I love doing things with people, for people. I'm much more content with this than being by myself. I'm happy with my life. Now I have a full bike with everything on it—and I'm sharing it."

Many of us don't ask for help because we think it is a sign of weakness. Asking for help is a strength. It is a sign that you are taking care of your own needs. Sit down and create a list of people who can help you feel less pressured. Problem-solving gives you control of the situation; it allows you to create your own positive environment amid the stress of everyday chaos.

Problem-solving is another technique that moves people into action. It gives control, versus staying stuck and complaining about the same old things.

## Gear-Shifting Action Steps

1. Write the name of a negative person who brings you down. Problem-solve a plan to protect yourself.

2. Who is a cheerleader in your life? What does this person do to encourage you?

3.  Who are you a cheerleader for? How do you encourage this person to be the best he or she can be?

4.  On the left side of a paper, make a list of the situations that troubled you last year. On the right side, list the effects of each situation. Hopefully the items on the right side won't seem so important.

    What worried me one year ago?
    What are the consequences?
    At work?
    At home?
    With relationships?

    Now make a list of the troubles you're facing today.
    Visualize how they will turn out one year from now.
    What worries me today?
    What will be the consequences?
    At work?
    At home?
    With relationships?

> **Live in the solution, not the problem.**
> – Og Mandino, author and professional speaker

# chapter 2

# Fun

## "Look Ma ... No Hands!"

## Give Yourself the Freedom to Have Fun

### Is Your Creativity on "Hold"?

In your company, do people get promoted or recognized when their initiative "rocks" the corporate boat? Are creative ideas rewarded?

If the answer to either or both of these questions is "yes," then creativity flourishes in your organization. If the answer is "no," then the rewards will still come, but you may have to look a little more closely for them.

One of the greatest creativity indicators within a company is its employees. Do they deliver what they promise, offer lots of suggestions, and take risks? I always ask groups to raise their hands if they think they are creative. Usually one or two people raise their hands. When I ask how many people solve problems pretty well, most of the hands go up.

We are all creative in our own way. We just need to give ourselves permission to call ourselves creative. My definition of creativity includes continually looking at life a little differently. Doing this will change your focus and help you solve problems in a whole new way.

> ## *Imagination is more important than knowledge.*
> – Albert Einstein, physicist

I was reminded to do this when I faced a terrible disappointment a few years ago. A production manager had asked me to create an eight-cassette tape program for her. She would cover all the costs, and I would do the work and receive copies of the tapes to sell at my programs. I thought this was a great opportunity, so I cleared my schedule for the next three months and recorded cassettes day and night. There were cassettes on communication, how to add more fun to your life, diversity, change, creativity, and much more.

When I finished the project, I was proud of my work and the commitment I had made. I also felt very relieved that this part of the project was over.

That same day, the owner of the company called me. I started telling her how excited I was about the results. She said she had some bad news, and I heard her say the words that still haunt me today: "Joyce, I hope this won't be too disappointing, but we're going bankrupt and won't be using your tapes. Have a nice day." Then she hung up.

At the time, I didn't calmly say to myself, "One day this will be a good thing. There will be an opportunity in the future arising from this disaster." Of course I didn't say these things! I was angry! Why couldn't she have told me before I put so much time and passion into the project?

My son, Ron, told me I was becoming the kind of person that I discuss in my "dealing with difficult people" program. He told me he thought I was playing victim just a little too long. He asked me what I said to my audiences during the creativity programs. I said that when we are experiencing a challenge, we must take it and look at it a different way. There are many right answers, not just one. I also suggest people look at their situation as if they were using a camera. Change the focus and maybe a better picture will appear, or at least a more interesting one.

My son suggested I follow my own advice. I did and, with a new perspective, discovered I had eight chapters of a book that I had always wanted to write! My first book, *Full Speed Ahead: Become Driven by Change,* grew from that huge disappointment. By using the word "readers" instead of "listeners," in one week I created a book. I was able to see a dream come true after being prodded to look at a challenge in a new way.

Creativity is the ability to look at the same thing everyone else sees, yet notice something different. I think of it as playing the "what-if" game. The multi-million-dollar economy in Silicon Valley was inspired by "What if we shrink computer chips?"

Think of your own challenge: product or service. What if you shrink it, enlarge it, change its shape, add something, subtract something, or change the name? It's always fun to try the impossible because there is less competition. If everyone says you are wrong, you are one step ahead. If everyone laughs at you, you are way ahead of the pack.

I own a "PHD" camera, also known as "Push Here Dummy." It has a great zoom lens and takes wonderful pictures. Still, I wanted to learn to look at the world in a new way and take more interesting photos. I asked my friend, Monte Nagler, a fine art photographer who instructs advanced students, if I could join his class. Graciously, he encouraged me to attend.

> *There's really no secret to our approach. We keep moving forward—opening up new doors and doing new things because we're curious. And curiosity keeps leading us down new paths.*
>
> – Walt Disney, film animator

I learned so much about creativity in that class, especially that there is always more than one way to look at things.

One day, while I was in Mexico, I got ready to take a particular photograph. I had composed a scene with colorful flowers in front of a huge stained glass window. I was about to take the shot when a total stranger said, "It will never come out because of the glare of the sun." I ignored the comment and the photograph is one of the most beautiful scenes in my collection. My "PHD" camera was the same, yet my photographs changed because I observed the world with a fresh pair of eyes. I was even willing to take the risk that perhaps the picture would not come out.

I changed my personal focus, and took a better picture than I ever thought possible. That's what I'm saying in *Take the Ride of Your Life*. Do more than just live. Be creative and design the best ride possible. Take a detour and see where it will take you. Don't be afraid to try new things. Look at where you are on the road, instead of concentrating on the destination.

How about you? The next time a huge disappointment comes along, take a look through your "camera" and see if you can find a new perspective.

## Find a New Perspective

I have found that using improvisation techniques in my workshops works so well because there are no rules and, therefore, no mistakes. Teams can start over when they don't like where they are heading. Creativity increases because people have fun while adding their input to the exercises.

The results are fantastic. Preconceived notions evaporate, such as how certain things should be done quickly. Enthusiasm flows from the participants. Without the restriction of judgment, innovation flows. At the finish, silence represents reflection instead of inhibition.

Make sure you use "igniter phrases" when you share ideas with your group. Igniter phrases include: "Keep talking. You're on the right track. We can do a lot with that idea. That's great. How can we do it? I'm glad you brought that up. Look out world, here we come!"

At the same time, make sure you keep the "killer phrases" out of the creativity process. Comments like "It won't work" or "You've got to be kidding!" will stop the ideas flowing immediately.

Brainstorming is effective and exciting, yet many people miss the importance of "alone time." Creativity is an individual phenomenon, not a group activity. Every individual gets stimuli from the team through words and body language, but all new ideas come from time spent alone in contemplation. Creative ideas are most often found during more serene moments. When the new idea is presented to the team, others can then build upon the product of your alone time and make it even more successful.

Individual makeup is another important element of creative brainstorming. Some people are idea people; they have endless ideas, energy, and enthusiasm. Others like to play with the idea and make it better. They find flaws, or ask what is good about it. These people take a concept and shape it into reality. Still others

"IT'S NICE OF YOU TO CARRY MY BOOKS HOME
FOR ME, ROY."

take this refined idea and decide the next step for putting the idea into action. Everyone has a talent to bring forth, and we all require some alone time to put our talents to good use.

We all know people who have great ideas but never do anything with them. That is why it is so important to have different kinds of people working on a project. The process becomes richer and more interesting when individual strengths are added to the mix.

There are things you can do to stimulate your own imagination. Sit next to someone you don't know. Invite someone you'd like to get to know better to lunch. Solicit an opinion from someone you have never asked before. Or take care of a child for a few hours—you'll be amazed at how creative you can be.

Creativity is not something magical. It is very simple. It is a moment when you look at the ordinary and see the extraordinary. Start looking at your own life a little differently. You'll be delighted at the surprises and the rewards waiting for you.

## Keep Laughing: It Will Keep You Sane

If life is a creative journey, laughter is the shock absorber. Life is tough and frustrating at times. The world is not fair. People who know how to laugh have a terrific survival skill. Laughter helps you remain creative under pressure and stay healthier in the process.

I don't go to bed until I write down a humorous personal story or quote that made me smile during the day in my humor journal. It keeps my creative pump primed.

At times people are so stressed out they forget to give themselves permission to laugh. There is a big difference between being stupid and being silly. Dense and dumb are two synonyms for stupid. Silly means to be happy, prosperous, and innocent. Sounds pretty good to me. In my workshops, I ask people to tell each other their favorite food, game, or clothing fad they remember from childhood. The room always lights up with laughter and bright smiles. How about bringing out your inner child again?

Nowadays, when I'm on my bike, I seek puddles and splash right through them. Doing this gives me a fabulous sense of independence, and it makes me laugh. How about giving yourself permission to do something that made you laugh as a child?

As a young boy, Dr. Seuss drew flying cows in school. His teacher scolded him and told him to draw the world as it was or he would never be an artist. It is a good thing for all of us that he drew the world as he saw it. He always asked the question, "What would happen if?" And the answers were marvelously silly. He said, "If you could look at a situation when it is out of whack then you could see how it could be in whack. I prefer to look at things through the wrong end of the telescope."

> **Life literally abounds in comedy if you just look around you.**
>
> – Mel Brooks, filmmaker

Children are wonderful teachers. My grandchildren have taught me how to look at the commonplace and see it as something special. Children are adventurous, amazed, carefree, curious, enthusiastic, fearless, funny, natural, playful, and wondering.

To tap into that freedom once again, get some index cards and write one of the above words on each one. When you need a pick-me-up, choose a card. As you go about your grown-up day, see how many opportunities you can discover or create to express the specific childlike quality you selected. You won't sacrifice your adult status when you act childlike. You will increase your capacity to have more fun and enjoy your life. And I guarantee you will smile a whole lot more.

## Reset Your Funny Bone

A few years ago, I consulted a humor coach about ways to make my programs more fun and entertaining. She said humor is a skill anyone can learn; we just need to be more aware of all the funny things that happen to us. She suggested I write something funny that happened to me every day. It took a while to train myself to do this, but once I got the hang of it, it was easy. Now, for instance, if a person is rude to me, I look for the humor in that incident and record it in my journal. I also cut cartoons out of the paper and paste them in my journal for a quick "laugh fix" whenever I need it. Humor is the best stress-reliever I know.

Tune up *your* funny bone. Humor *is* all around you! Just because you may not perceive comical things happening at the time, doesn't mean they aren't there. Here are some real episodes that workshop participants have shared with me:

✦ Six-year-old Johnny asked his mother where he came from. The mom was very concerned, because she was not prepared to give her son "the talk" about the birds and bees quite yet. All of a sudden Johnny said, "Susie is from Detroit, where am I from?" Johnny's mom breathed a sigh of relief and told her six-year-old he came from Savannah.

✦ A client told me she was once given an award that she still laughs about. On the way down from the platform, she tripped and broke the toe of the person who gave her the huge trophy. This award was for being the manager of the safest department in the corporation.

✦ A new employee at a large company walked up to a paper shredder and stood before it looking confused. A team member asked, "Need some help?" She said, "Yes, how does this thing work?" "It's simple," he said as he took the thick report from his colleague's hand and fed it into the shredder. "See?" he asked. "I see," she said, "but how many copies will it make?"

✦ A tech support professional told me about the following conversation she had with a client.

Client: "Now what do I do?"

Tech: "What is the prompt on the screen?"

Client: "It's asking to enter your last name."

Tech: "OK. Do it."

Client: "How do you spell your last name?"

✦ I can add a story, too. I was the keynote speaker at an awards banquet. When I called out the name of a man to give him an award for his perfect attendance, he was not there. You can imagine the audience response.

## Gear-Shifting Action Steps

1. Spend a day paying attention to how receptive you are to new ideas. On a scale of 1 to 10, how would you rate your open-mindedness? Do you immediately disregard other ideas, play devil's advocate, or do you really consider what's being suggested? Do you listen without judgment until the idea is fully explained, or do you begin a silent rebuttal, waiting for your turn to speak?

2. Make a list of fifteen things you do for personal enjoyment. Once you have made this list, ask yourself when you last did some of these activities. Decide which are the most important and make plans to enjoy doing them again. Schedule them in your planner now!

3. You are the artist of your life, with the necessary talents to create masterpieces. Unleash your natural strengths and skills to create the best you can be. Have fun with these activities and watch a colorful work of art take form.

   ✦ Keep a journal to record your insights.
   ✦ Take adequate time for self-reflection.
   ✦ Enjoy learning something new.
   ✦ Learn from children and adults.
   ✦ Try to be more open-minded and curious.

Remember: the little kid inside of you is a super-creative resource for you. You deserve fun and pleasure.

> ### *Humor is tragedy plus time.*
> – Mark Twain, author

# chapter 3

# Obstacles

## "Where Did That #@! Car Door Come From?!"

## How to Safely Navigate Life's Potholes, Ruts, and Obstacles

Learning life's lessons only through positive experiences would be terrific. But, life isn't that way for a good reason. Negative experiences teach us to use failure as a learning tool. We wouldn't be who we are if we didn't live through the unique good and bad lessons that teach us what we need to know.

### "What's in a Bike?"— More Stories of Triumph

**SALLY**

Sally learned a wonderful lesson the positive way. Her first bike experience didn't take place until after she was married. It made a strong impression. "During the Depression," she recalls, "none of us had any money. People made do then. It was a simpler time. I never had my own bike or a chance to ride one.

"One day, we went to River Rouge for a picnic and saw that there were bicycles to rent. My husband taught me how to ride. He was so gentle! I trusted him completely. Before I knew it, I was off and riding. In a way, this event sums up what I believe: When I want to do something, I do it, right then and there. I don't wait or plan for the perfect time. I seize the opportunity when it's there.

"Now I'm in my eighties and am an independent widow. I don't want to trouble anyone else if I can help it. When the faucet broke, I went to the hardware store, bought a new one, and replaced the old one. It gave me a lot of satisfaction. Although I haven't been bike riding in a while, I exercise every day. When I go places with my daughters, I can keep up with them. I still drive a car, so I still 'pedal' —even if it's with one foot."

Sally does not complain very often, and has no patience with those who do. Upbeat, non-judgmental, and full of enthusiasm, she's always ready to learn new things, because every day offers her new opportunities, despite obstacles.

## Everybody Makes Mistakes

Here's an important lesson I learned from a shocking event in my life. In 1993, I received the Certified Speaking Professional (CSP) designation, the highest certification you can earn from the National Speakers Association (NSA). It recognized my commitment to ongoing education, proven speaking experience, and ethical behavior. Of the 3,500 members of the NSA, only 7% have attained the CSP designation.

At my proudest moment, however, I made a serious error. I started believing the hype about what a talented speaker I was, and this was my downfall. I had to learn this the hard way.

After I received the CSP designation, I was looking forward to giving a keynote address at an awards convention. I believed the audience would be honored to have a certified speaking professional address them. I spoke for five minutes and 3,000—I repeat, 3,000—people walked out of the room! I was in shock, and the meeting planner was horrified.

> *Good judgment comes from experience and experience comes from bad judgment.*
>
> – Mark Twain, author

"*I'M RUNNING AWAY FROM HOME AND THIS IS MY SIXTEENTH TIME AROUND THE BLOCK. MOM WON'T LET ME CROSS THE STREET.*"

Believe me, I quickly started learning a lot about myself that night. I learned that I am human and vulnerable. I make mistakes. After I recovered from my embarrassment, I continued this learning process by honestly evaluating the experience, the people involved, and all the reactions. It took me a while to sift out the answer to the question, "Joyce, what in the world did you do to make 3,000 people walk out?"

First I blamed the time of day—right after lunch—wanting to assume that people were full and tired. It's easy to look toward others, instead of into ourselves for explanations of failure.

Then I did a candid assessment of the situation. I had not researched the group ahead of time as I usually do. I did not tailor my presentation for my audience. One of the things my clients compliment me for is how much I know about their organization. This audience was new to the customer service industry, but I did not know this. I had dismissed doing my homework because I thought I was good enough, that I was "already there."

> *Those who do not learn from the past are condemned to repeat it. The trick is to turn common sense into common practice.*
>
> – George Santayana, philosopher

My second mistake was not going to bed early enough. I figured that I was now a certified speaking professional. Why should I have to prepare when I was already at the peak of my career? I was resting on my laurels.

I learned a final important lesson from this experience. The night before I came home, I called my husband, Jerry, to tell him what had happened and how devastated I felt. When I returned home, I walked into my kitchen and found a beautiful bouquet of flowers with a card that read, "You may have bombed at your speech, but you are still dynamite with me."

That card brought me back to reality. I finally understood that although I needed to take my career seriously, I also needed to lighten up and see that life is more than just work. I had to put my experience into perspective and learn to accept it with the support of the ones I love.

The next time something devastating happens to you, I hope you will remember that there are lessons to be learned. I'm not saying you shouldn't savor the moment or enjoy your achievements, awards, and compliments. Enjoy them; just make sure you don't stay stuck in the "I'm the greatest" mode. Don't make the mistake of thinking that since you are "already there" you don't have to try as hard. The truth is you must try even harder.

Most importantly, recognize the great friends and family who support you during your up-and-down times. We are normally very hard on ourselves, and our personal support systems really bring perspective. Life is tough enough; why not treat yourself just a little easier?

## FRAN

For Fran, living with multiple sclerosis (MS) offers new challenges each day, a reality she has faced for the nineteen years since her diagnosis. At one very difficult period, Fran had to learn to use a wheelchair and a walker. She had to relearn using a fork and holding a glass. Like a child, she had to be shown how to dress herself. Nonetheless, she always sees opportunities.

"In this kind of situation, you do appreciate a lot more and see things differently," she says. "For instance, I recently bought a flat of mixed flowers because I was determined to plant my own garden full of color. To do this, I had to sit on a special stool with my tools piled in a wheelbarrow next to me. It gave me a great sense of accomplishment to plant those flowers all by myself and watch them bloom."

In the same way, Fran feels it is important to teach her children to stand on their own two feet and be independent. "I want to educate them to have both strength and sensitivity because, sadly, these are two qualities that my parents didn't have in great abundance."

When Fran and her husband were first married, they rode matching green Schwinn bikes side by side. Today she "pedals on" with the help of a turquoise walker, a supportive husband, three children, and a great attitude. She even uses an electric scooter to accompany her husband while he runs. Strength and sensitivity are her constant companions. "I told myself I could be depressed all the time and feel sorry for myself, or I could acknowledge that I have a lot to live for, which I do."

## JOANNE

Joanne also believes that opportunities always exist, either despite of or because of physical challenges. In 1992, when she was a college student, Joanne suffered a serious accident. She fell from her loft bed, landed on a metal-framed lounger, and broke her back. Several surgeries and a demanding regimen of physical therapy followed. With enormous concentration and effort, she was able to return to college the following fall.

> *Happy people feel that they can direct the course of their own lives and get where they are going, even though the going may be rough. People who are obsessed with their mistakes, who are stuck on the missed opportunity of the past, have no time to be happy. The past is unchangeable. Trying to change it is the source of most unhappiness.*
>
> – Sherwin T. Wine, Founder, The Center for New Thinking

"I was still suffering from paralysis so I bought a hand cycle. I ride it through the parks here as often as I can," she says. "It reminds me of being a little girl in Connecticut where I rode a four-wheeled scooter. My parents always helped guide me down the big hill by our house. When we moved to Michigan, I received my first two-wheeler bike. It had a purple frame and plastic tires. My father taught me how to ride it. He encouraged me, telling me to stay focused and concentrate. My mother, on the other hand, told me to be very careful. I rode along dirt roads and paths through the neighborhood. Sometimes I went up to the store with my friends. I loved the freedom of riding my bike.

"Now I'm teaching a little girl how to ride a hand cycle. I tell her to stay focused and concentrate, just like my father told me when he taught me how to ride my first bike."

Joanne, now a research engineer, recognized another special opportunity after her injury. Today she serves as the volunteer regional director for the Buoniconti Fund to Cure Paralysis.

### NINA

Nina, an insurance agent, has her own unique story. At age sixteen, she was diagnosed with scoliosis, or "curvature of the spine" as it is commonly called. She had to wear a back brace for six months. This was followed by spinal surgery. Afterwards, she wore a body cast for eight months. "It was disappointing," she remembers. "Since I was five years old I had taken gymnastics—and I was good. After my illness, gymnastics, along with any varsity sport, was out of the question. But with strength and determination, I put my energy into other activities, like becoming class president. I figure if something ends in one area of your life, you can always do another thing—and succeed at it, too."

Recently, Nina taught her five-year-old daughter how to ride a bike. It brought back memories of her own first ride. "Old memories of learning to ride came right back to me. I told my daughter the same things that I was told by my parents."

When Nina's son was four, she and her husband took the training wheels off his bike. "He had a big fall, so we put the training wheels back on. Now he rides a brand new bike—a two-wheeler—and he is so proud of himself," says Nina. He takes after his mom. Just as Nina fell off her bike and persevered, today she keeps moving forward, always looking ahead to new challenges.

"I have to put forth great effort in anything I really want to do. But I will always succeed if I work hard enough and want it. The opportunity to accomplish something new is always there."

## Let Your Mistakes Teach You

Learn quickly from your mistakes and move on. Beating yourself up over and over again doesn't help you or anybody else.

How would you rate yourself in reference to each of the following statements?

+ I am willing to acknowledge my mistakes.
  ❑ Always   ❑ Sometimes   ❑ Rarely

+ I learn from my mistakes.
  ❑ Always   ❑ Sometimes   ❑ Rarely

+ i rarely make the same mistake twice.
  ❑ Always   ❑ Sometimes   ❑ Rarely

## Seek New Opportunities

Here's a very telling tale about a coal miner. This coal miner, stuck in a mine shaft with no way out, was feeling desperate. All of a sudden he heard a whoosh, and a genie appeared. She told the miner to take as many pieces of coal as he could and put them in his pockets before he went to sleep. If he did this, she said, he would feel both happy and sad when he woke up the next morning. The man was very tired, but he listened to the genie and managed to pick up a few pieces of coal before he went to sleep.

The next morning when he awoke, he was out of the coal mine and back in his bed. He was very happy to be out of the coal mine. When he reached into his pocket to pull out the coal, he found it had been changed into diamonds. He suddenly felt sad, because he had only taken a few pieces of coal.

Just like the coal miner, we need to give even the worst situation in life a chance to reveal its greatness. Even if we don't immediately see any opportunities, we need to learn all we can about the situation, then begin seeking out those "diamonds in the rough" and trusting that we will find them.

### MEL

At age 51, Mel started a new business and relates this latest venture to riding his secondhand bike on the city streets as a child. "That Schwinn was my only transportation. I was always running errands for my mother, going to the store to pick up a loaf of bread or a container of milk. I also used the bike for my paper route.

*Far away in the sunshine are my highest aspirations. I may not reach them, but I can look up and see the beauty, believe in them, and try to follow where they lead.*

– Louisa May Alcott, author

"Now I realize that that bike bridged a connection between who I am and my experience with a larger world. It represented opportunity, one that I took full advantage of. That old bike provided fun, transportation, and helped me earn money. Consequently, I've continued to see exciting new opportunities around me all my life."

## JACK

Jack is also a man who knows how to see an opportunity when it comes along. After thirty years in a successful pediatric practice, he decided to leave. "I couldn't agree with the policies of the new management," he relates. "I'm not a big risk taker, but I know what's right and what isn't right for me.

"I got my first bike when I was a teenager, right after World War II," says Jack. "The bike was neat, a brand new maroon Roadmaster with a front light. My father kept reminding me to be careful because the streets were too narrow to accommodate cars and bicycles at the same time. It wasn't as if he had to remind me, though. I never forgot a terrible incident that happened when I was three years old. I saw a playmate get hit and killed by a car. I had been afraid of traffic ever since.

"For me, riding my bike was an opportunity to overcome that fear. Today I understand that you still have to 'go out in traffic'—out into the flow of life. You may avoid disaster by staying on the sidelines, but you'll also miss out on all the opportunities out there. I know now that wherever there are risks, there are also rewards.

"Nowadays I'm 'retired' from my practice, but I still teach medical students. Every day *does* offer fresh experiences."

When will you become yourself? Many people would rather hold on to the past and feel sorry for the way things are. They cry about what they do not get, not realizing that they can create their own journeys.

## Fear: It's Not Worth Worrying About

**KRISTEN**

Kristen, who owns a speakers' bureau, created her own journey despite the fact that, much of the time, it wasn't easy. When she was a child, her father told her, "Learn how to ride your bike yourself." He then gave her one forceful shove, and walked away.

With an emotionally distant father and an insecure mother, Kristen had a lot to deal with. But she was also fortunate because her loving grandmother became her role model. "She gave me incredible gifts," Kristen remembers. "A sense of adventure was one. The importance of helping others was yet another. She showed me how honesty, integrity, authenticity, faith, perseverance, kindness, and forgiveness could make an impact in my everyday life."

As a single parent, Kristen now encourages her three children not to be afraid. "Make it happen," she tells them, remembering how she learned to ride her bike herself. Yet she's also there to support them in that journey.

Kristen overcame her disappointment in her father's behavior and has tapped into her inner strength to help others. "Someone once asked me what changes I would make if I was to relive my life. I don't think that way. Everything I have done or been through has made me who I am. If I truly love who I am, then I have only thanks for my past."

## Even Fear Can Lead to Opportunities

It took me more than a decade to learn one of my most important life lessons. My business was growing and I thought it was going to always be that way. Therefore, I did marketing the same way for ten years. I sent my past clients PR materials a few times a year and did what I could to get new business. I attended networking opportunities, such as Chamber of Commerce and other professional association meetings that my prospects also attended.

One day the phone stopped ringing, and my appointment

> *Don't listen to anyone who tells you that you can't do this or that. That's nonsense. Make up your mind, you'll never use crutches or a stick, then have a go at everything. Go to school; join in all the games you can. Go anywhere you want to. But never, never let them persuade you that things are too difficult or impossible.*
>
> – Sir Douglas Bader, World War II British pilot who previously lost both legs in a flying accident. The above quote is from a talk he had with a 14-year-old boy who lost his leg in an auto accident. He was later knighted for his work with the physically challenged.

book began looking pretty empty. What in the world was happening? I was afraid my business would fail, yet kept doing things the same way, knowing something was wrong.

After one year of total fear, I finally decided to analyze the situation. I met with some other speakers, and we shared our concerns. Some speakers were struggling, while others were having their best year ever. I took notes during these meetings and found my answer. Many of the loyal professionals who had hired me in the past were no longer working. They had either been downsized out of their jobs or retired. No wonder the phone had stopped ringing! The answer was so simple, yet not knowing it had kept me paralyzed with fear for a whole year!

Realizing that I had to do something totally different with my marketing, I started calling past clients to get them excited about some of the new programs I had added. If they were not the decision-makers anymore, I made sure to ask who was. I began advertising on the Internet and hired the very talented web site designer, Julie Hunkar, to design a web site for me. I started networking with colleagues and actively engaged referrals to generate reciprocal business.

> **The average human looks without seeing and listens without hearing.**
>
> – Leonardo Da Vinci, Renaissance artist

I made a list of people who are my advocates and cheerleaders. These people have been a great source of referrals for me in the past. Plus, they believe in what I do. I send these supporters small gifts and notes every few months and the response has been extremely positive. Because they understand how much I value them, they are happy to refer their new contacts to me. It's a win-win opportunity!

Ultimately, I didn't let fear get the best of me because I looked for the facts I needed to make changes.

### JODI

Jodi, a physical therapist, understands overcoming fear. She can trace her self-confidence to the day she gave up the training wheels on her blue-and-white striped bike. "I told my dad I was ready, but allowing him to let go of the bike took some doing," she says. "He kept telling me not to look back, not to worry about him. My job was to keep pedaling and look straight ahead. When I finally rode by myself, my confidence soared."

This confidence never wavered, not even when she suffered a closed head injury, the result of a car accident at age seventeen. Her recovery was difficult and frustrating, but Jodi persevered.

"My grades dropped, and I did not do well on the SAT college entrance exams. The hardest part was that I would jumble words and forget things. Nonetheless, I managed to achieve my long-standing goal of attending the University of Michigan. I graduated with honors, but to this day I still have residual deficits from the accident.

"I want to pass on the lessons I've learned. My dad taught me to ride that striped bike with gentleness and kindness. I will tell my kids there are three 'you can do it' lessons: Family is very important. Be loyal to your friends. Never give up."

## Facing Your Fear

What actions can you take to make sure that fear will not take over and destroy you?

Who can you talk to for help in breaking out of your status quo?

Ask yourself: Do I want to be a lump of coal, or do I want to be a diamond?

### LUMP-OF-COAL BELIEFS:

1. This kind of thing always happen to me.
2. It's not fair.
3. If it's risky, I shouldn't do it.

### LUMP-OF-COAL ACTIONS:

1. Give up.
2. Take things out on others.
3. Let fear stop me or keep me stuck.

### DIAMOND BELIEFS:

1. I can make this work for me.
2. I can be open to possibilities.
3. I can handle it and enjoy the process.

### DIAMOND ACTIONS:

1. Live a life of fulfillment.
2. Confront fears head-on.
3. Make fear work for me.

Remember: Diamonds are made from coal. Like the coal miner, give the obstacles a chance to present their diamond opportunity.

## Gear-Shifting Action Steps

1.  What pluses have come from your negative experiences?

    You may need to dig deep, but be assured, you will find a lesson.

2.  Are there areas where you have inherited potential-blocking behaviors and attitudes similar to those of your family members?

    Awareness is a great first step to stopping behaviors that you don't like in others.

3.  Which of your own dreams or beliefs have you put aside in order to fulfill the expectations of others?

    It's time to live the life you deserve.

4.  What do you need to let go of to finally grow up?

    Stop putting the blame on your parents or siblings. Accepting total self-responsibility is an empowering feeling.

5.  What is the biggest mistake you ever made and what did you learn from it?

    This book is full of my own mistakes. I have learned to trust myself when I fall down, knowing that getting back up is just as natural a part of life.

6.  What did your parents teach you about making mistakes?

    Either they made you feel guilty or they encouraged you to learn from your errors. If your situation is the former, then it's time to let go of the guilt.

7.  Both in the past and the present, what parts of yourself have you hidden from others for fear they would disapprove of you? What parts do you hide even from yourself?

Once you are determined to take off your training wheels, you'll be amazed at what you will discover about yourself!

# chapter 4

# **Authenticity**

## "I Don't Care What You Think: I Want That Purple Bike!"

## Know Who You Are to Get What You Want

Being authentic is about being yourself—that is, connecting with your natural self. When you are authentic, you can identify both your values and what it takes to live by them. When this happens, you can make life really work for you.

Success in life isn't just about getting and having more; it's about becoming your authentic self in every facet of your life. Feeling satisfied and reaching your potential are both part of that fulfillment equation.

### "What's in a Bike?"— More Stories of Triumph

**ROSS**

Ross, a consultant, understands what being true to oneself means. Growing up on a farm gave him lots of opportunities to find out what had meaning for him. The rule of hard work was part of everday life, and one that has served him well. "My father always said, 'Work hard and be ethical. Don't try to manipulate people or situations.' This advice has shaped me as much as the wonderful memories of picking the first strawberries, blackberries, and blueberries each summer. Whenever I smell lilacs, no matter where I am, I recall my parents, how hard they worked, and how honest they were.

"They couldn't buy me a new bike. No one I knew ever had one. It seemed everyone had a hand-me-down. When I was eight, I learned to ride a bike with a twenty-six-inch frame. My legs were so short my feet didn't even touch the ground," he recalls. "Still, I taught myself how to do it.

"I had a great incentive," he says. "Whenever I walked to the mailbox — it was about a mile away — I was always scared of the neighbor's bull. I had been chased more than once. One day, when my mother asked me to get the mail, I looked at that bike and knew I had to figure out how to ride it. Our house was on top of a hill, and I thought I could coast for a while. And that's how I got started. When I got to the mailbox, I grabbed onto it to keep myself and the bike upright. Then I had to figure out how to get going again. I pushed off from the mailbox real hard. I kept the bike upright, and rode all the way home. It felt like a major accomplishment."

Today, Ross is an independent person who has discovered that setting his own work schedule is integral to who he is. "I could never work from nine to five and deal with freeway traffic twice a day," he declares. "To me, that's the adult equivalent of being chased by a bull every day. I would rather work sixteen hours a day doing what I want rather than force myself to work nine hours a day doing something I do not really care about."

## ELLEN

Ellen is another person who believes there is always room to learn and grow, a lesson she has taught her three children. "While I don't

> *He who controls others may be powerful, but he who has mastered himself is mightier still.*
>
> – Lao Tzu, philosopher and founder of Taoism

> **If I am not for myself, who will be for me? If I am not for others, what am I? And if not now, when?**
>
> – Rabbi Hillel, first century teacher

have a 'bike' story, I do recall a defining childhood event that involved being on wheels," she says. "My dad used to bundle me up and take me for rides in a little wagon. I can still recapture that special feeling of being protected. I think it contributed to my strong sense of who I am, as well as the belief that there is always opportunity to become more. Now my goal is to become more accepting and less critical, both of myself and of others. I see myself as a 'loving straight shooter' and wish to be accepted and remembered that way."

## Be Yourself: It's the Best You Can Be

When I gave the welcome speech at my thirty-fifth high school reunion, my message was very basic: Accept yourself, wherever you are in your life. I suggested that my former classmates go up to people they had never spoken with, or had ignored thirty-five years ago, and just enjoy the experience.

The result was wonderful. People told me it was the best reunion they had ever attended, because they could be authentic. They knew who they were and they didn't have to impress old classmates. Getting along was a whole lot easier because people who know themselves are a pleasure to be with. They are comfortable with their strengths and weaknesses. They do not play victim. They accept who they are and feel confident that they can do whatever it takes to keep getting better.

My reunion was interesting to me personally, because some of the people attending told me they had regarded me as a kind of "coach," even back then. It reminded me that one way to identify a natural strength is to listen to others when they talk about what they see in you. We all have natural blind spots about ourselves. In high school, for example, I had no inkling that I would be

> *I was told over and over again that I would never be successful, that I was not going to be competitive, and the technique was simply not going to work. All I could do was shrug and say, "We'll just see."*
>
> – Dick Fosbury, Olympic gold medalist and inventor of a revolutionary high-jump technique

doing the kind of work I do. So pay attention to what is offered by others.

Being true to yourself is a commitment to being authentic, and not trying to be somebody you are not. I discovered this a few years ago when I decided to go to a drama coach to get help in tightening up my stories.

Having observed other speakers, I thought I would be more successful if I became like them. Their stories were full of flair and told with very dramatic gestures. My coach helped me develop these different techniques, and I was excited about the "new" Joyce that was evolving.

About a year after my sessions with the drama coach, some of my colleagues saw me give a presentation. They told me that I was not myself and asked what had happened to my creativity and spontaneity. At first, I dismissed their comments. The new me was evolving, I thought; they just didn't understand. One day, a colleague from the speakers' bureau took me aside and was as honest as she could be. She said I had been a better speaker a few years ago and told me she was concerned about the direction I was taking.

What she said brought home to me that I was trying to be someone I was not. While we all need role models, we must retain our own unique style. The minute we become what we are not, we lose our authenticity. Today I don't worry about where to stand or which arm to extend when I'm making a point. I just let me be me.

## AHMED

Ahmed, a web developer, learned to ride his bike when he was ready. At thirteen, he was a "late bloomer" where bike riding was concerned. Nonetheless, he remembers that his father and friends gave him a lot of encouragement.

"The first time I got on the bike—a little orange Road Runner one-speed with black handles and a banana seat—I rode it, which amazed and delighted me. I continue to find, all these years later, that you can't rush things. You have to be true to yourself, know which things need to be done when you are ready, and which ones you have to do at a particular moment. Being true to myself means asking myself which kind of situation I'm in, and then determining the outcome."

"HE WAS A GREAT GENERAL, BUT AFRAID OF HORSES — "

> *Ninety percent of the world's woes come from people not knowing themselves, their abilities, their frailties, and even their real virtues. Most of us go almost all the way through life as complete strangers to ourselves.*
>
> – Sydney J. Harris, newspaper columnist

## SUE

Sue, a registered nurse, says, "Having nursing skills gives me the confidence to know I can help people any time they need it.

"I always had high expectations for myself, and sometimes these worked against me. Now I understand that they are part of who I am. I also understand that, like the training wheels I had on my first bike, and my older brother guiding me when those wheels came off, I need a supportive environment. That is part of who I am, too. At the same time, I realize that as I get older, people expect me to be independent, to do everything on my own. That doesn't work for me. I find that revealing my 'human' side allows people to see the real me, which is important."

One of my favorite children's books is *The Velveteen Rabbit*, written by Margery Williams. The toy horse's description of being real rings true for all of us:

> "Generally, by the time you are Real most of your hair has been loved off, and your eyes drop out and you get loose in the joints and very shabby. But these things don't matter at all, because once you are Real you can't be ugly, except to people who don't understand."

## MARTY

Marty, a general contractor, has felt authentic since he was a boy climbing on his first bike, a Schwinn. "I outfitted it with horns, flares, crash bars — all sorts of things," he remembers. "I lived in a great Detroit neighborhood, filled with alleys that served as playgrounds for football, baseball, or whatever was in season. Everyone was friendly, and we all traded fantasies about what we would become when we grew up."

Riding came easily to Marty, which set the tone for succeeding as an adult. "I never take lessons," he says. "Most of the stuff I learn is by trial and error or by watching. I like to learn through practical experience. My philosophy is simple: You get one shot at life. Do the best you can with it and enjoy it. I've had phenomenal experiences because I followed the path of who I am."

## LISA

Lisa's authenticity comes from following her heart, a fitting path for the stepdaughter of a cardiologist. "My father and mother told me I could do anything, including, of course, riding a bicycle," the public relations entrepreneur recollects. "Getting on that bike and being able to move faster than I ever had before was a very powerful feeling. When I let go of the handlebars the first time and pushed through the wind, everything and everybody sped by. It was an incredibly exhilarating experience! I was a kid who needed to be free, and the feeling never left me."

Her great spirit of independence can be daunting. "It's not easy, and it doesn't make you popular, to be independent. I've found that people who see me as someone following her own path tend to challenge me."

> *Sometimes you have to play a long time to be able to play like yourself.*
> – Miles Davis, musician

The dual feelings of confidence and taking a chance are defining aspects of Lisa's personality. "In my twenties I began to ask, 'Whose life is this anyway?' This is my life! No matter what I do, some people will judge me. I might as well do the thing I want most, especially when there are 'bumps' in the road to where I'm going."

## Be Yourself and Please Yourself

People feel so confident when they find their real selves. They can be true to their own personality and feel comfortable, even when others choose not to accept them. There is no price you can put on such a feeling.

Recently, my husband and I were having dinner with long-time friends and a couple we had never met before. I was talking about the progress of this book and my excitement about it.

Finally, the man I had not met before said to me, "Joyce, are you always this passionate and optimistic about things? Your enthusiasm is pouring out all over the table. Have you always been like this, or is it an acquired skill?"

Both my husband and I got the impression that my authentic self was a bit much for him. This man could not understand my passion. That's okay. We can never please everyone. He does not need to accept me or be sensitive to why I feel so strongly about things. I bring this up in all my keynote speeches because so many people try to be accepted by everyone. That is an exercise in frustration. I feel my enthusiasm and optimism are two of my strengths. Let's face it: Have you ever heard of a motivational speaker who is low-energy? I don't think so!

Anytime we take our strengths and overuse them, however, they become weaknesses. I know I have to tone down my energy at times. I realize that optimism needs to be served with a huge dose of reality every once in a while. But to know your strengths and to be true to yourself is important, even if others do not always think you're okay.

Here are a few examples of strengths and their related weaknesses. Being a good listener is a real plus. It can become a weakness, however, when others want your opinion or input, and you have nothing to offer. Being detail-oriented is also a must for most organizations today. Unfortunately, you can become bogged down in trivia if you let this strength be overpowering. Having a strong personality is another asset, but it can rapidly become a weakness if your behavior constantly overshadows other people around you.

I have a trademark registered with the government. It is:

> *"The magic within you is no hocus pocus.*
> *Set your goals and you create the focus."*

The more we know about ourselves, the more we focus on the strengths and talents we have right inside. With this knowledge, we become more complete. We just have to give ourselves permission to look and take the time to find it.

### SUZIE

Suzie, a psychotherapist, took the time she needed. Throughout her life she has pedaled forward with caution. "I'm the kind of person who doesn't like new situations," she admits. "I get anxious. If I can hold onto something familiar until I get my bearings, then I can let go and fly. This is exactly the situation I had when I learned to ride a bicycle at age eight.

> **If a man does not keep pace with his companions,**
> **perhaps it is because he hears a different drummer.**
> **Let him step to the music he hears, however**
> **measured or far away.**
>
> – Henry David Thoreau, poet

Once upon a time Buddha called a great gathering of his leaders. He was feeling very frustrated. He said, "People are taking wisdom for granted. They think it is nothing. They don't appreciate its value. We must take wisdom from them and hide it where it will not be found. Where shall we hide it?"

One of the leaders said, "I know, Buddha. Let's put it on top of the highest mountain." Buddha thought for a moment, and replied, "Good suggestion. My concern, however, is that people will learn how to climb mountains. Where else can we hide wisdom?"

Another leader said, "Let's bury it in the deepest ocean." Again Buddha thought and replied, "That is another good idea. But I'm concerned that people will figure out how to dive. I know: let's hide it inside people. They will never think of looking within. They will never find it there."

All of us are in the same situation. So much of what we need to know is within ourselves. We already have the answers. We just have to use our own magic to find it in our own way.

"My father was a grocer who worked long hours. He bought me a blue bike with silver trim and taught me how to ride. He held the back of the bike and told me to pedal very fast. More importantly, he kept telling me, 'You are safe. I won't let go!' "

Suzie's life took a dramatic turn when she was twelve. Her father suffered a life-threatening heart attack, which altered the way her parents thought about what women should or should not do. "The rather radical notion that women had to learn to take care of themselves gave me the gift of independence."

For Suzie, learning how to ride her bicycle represents several defining characteristics, including freedom, growth, risk-taking, and moving into the world. Today, she still rides her bike to the store, and experiences those positive feelings every time she does so.

**STEPHEN**

Stephen, an attorney who learned to ride his bike as a symbolic escape from homework and family obligations, found himself, too—but it took a while. "I tried a lot of careers," he says. "Engineering, law, teaching—I tried them all. Until I did, I didn't realize that law was the right one. Sometimes that happens. You have to try things to see what does or doesn't 'fit' with who you are. One thing I do know: When I ride my bike at night, alone, I feel free. You can't be judged when you're riding your bike."

## Gear-Shifting Action Steps

1. What lessons did your parents teach you?

2. What lessons do you feel are important to teach your kids or nieces/nephews?

3. What natural skills do others say you possess? Start listening—you may be pleasantly surprised.

4. What do you think you do best? Translate this into other areas of your life.

5. What people, places, and activities allow you to feel most fully yourself?

6. Write down things that were dreams at one time and that you made into a reality.

7.  What have been the important experiences in your life and what have you learned from them? Start writing your own story. Include a "Who's Who" description for each decade to capture where you've been in your life and to appreciate where you are right now.

    Up to age 9
    10–19
    20–29
    30–39
    40–49
    50–59
    60–69
    70–90

8.  What are your weaknesses, blind spots, or areas for improvement?

9.  How do you want to be remembered?

10. How can you get paid to do something you love to do? George Burns said, "Do something you love and now go and get paid for it."

# chapter 5

# Straight Talk

## "Where the Heck Are We Anyway?"

### Take the Direct Route: Navigating by Communicating

## Create More Meaningful Relationships with Others—and Yourself

It takes courage to stand up and speak to others. It also takes courage to sit down and listen to yourself.

Are any of these negative thoughts part of your thinking process? "I look old." "This class is such a waste of time." "My neighborhood stinks." "What if I get lost?" "I'm no good at giving speeches." "I'm not looking forward to another boring evening." Thoughts like these can keep you stuck in a less-than-positive state of mind.

If you pay attention to your conversations, you will become aware of using phrases such as "I'll never," "I don't," "It's too hard," "I should have known better," "Yes, but." These words, and others like them, are self-sabotaging and stop you from taking action. Repeating these messages to others only adds fuel to the fire of your self-doubt. No one betrays you as much as you betray yourself by building these self-imposed "bumps" in the road of your life.

Many people undermine their own success, as well as their environment, by talking pessimistically to themselves and others. An effective way of combating negative habits is to network with others in order to find support during the ups and downs of life. For instance, my son and I continually challenge each other to break away from our own negative thoughts and behaviors and from negative people.

## Be Your Own Coach: Use Straight Talk

Using "straight talk" is a way to build rapport with others, solve issues, and create meaningful relationships. This means being honest about your feelings, without anger or accusation.

People know where they stand with me because there is no gray area, only black and white. You may think, "Joyce, this is a very brash statement to make." You are right; it *is* a very strong statement.

I haven't used straight talk all my life. At one time, I agreed with people just to agree. I wanted to please everyone. Eventually, I found that this was an impossible feat. Straight talk is an acquired skill that has changed my mental and physical health. When I don't use straight talk, I don't sleep well because I think about situations where I should have said or done something and didn't. Maybe the same thing happens to you.

Do you pretend the sarcastic comments your partner makes don't bother you? Do you silently listen while a friend judges someone you care about without defending that person? Do you smile when you really feel hurt? If so, you aren't being straight with yourself—much less anyone else.

> *All problems become smaller if you don't dodge them, but confront them.*
>
> – **William Halsey, US Naval Officer**

Buddha was known to be fair. People knew that he gave others a chance, no matter how tough the situation.

In a city far from Buddha there lived a man who loved challenging others with his sarcasm. He decided to find Buddha and see if he could make Buddha angry. When he found Buddha, the man was meaner than ever and did his best to challenge Buddha.

Buddha said, "If you give another man a gift and he does not accept it, to whom does the gift belong?" The man thought and said, "It would still belong to me, since I bought it." Buddha said, "You are right. Since you are trying to give me all your negativity and sarcasm, I will not accept it. Therefore, it still belongs to you."

The man went back to his home, angrier than ever before.

A number of people tell me that they want to learn straight talk but are afraid of the risks it involves. They would like to use straight talk with their boss yet fear it could backfire and make the situation worse. They want to be able to tell negative co-workers how their behavior brings down morale, yet feel the people involved would yell at them. They are upset with a family member but avoid being honest.

The reality is that it is a risk to show your vulnerability to others. This is why straight talk is one of the hardest skills to learn. It is also one of the most important ones, for one fundamental reason. Everyone, including yourself, ought to be told what they need to hear—not what they want to hear.

This is a new way of thinking and communicating for those who are used to holding things inside. Being direct and truthful builds self-confidence and will earn you respect from others as well. The more you use straight talk, the easier it becomes. Take time to practice what you really need to say; your investment will pay huge dividends.

I always advise managers to use straight talk because employees are often confused about what is expected of them. Straight talk outlines roles and jobs, creating a workplace where people know their parameters. Stress magically disappears when employees know they can depend on being treated with honesty.

## "What's in a Bike?"— More Stories of Triumph

### MICHELLE

Michelle, who is in sales and marketing, believes using straight talk is worth any risks it may involve. "Straight talk is a skill everyone should learn," she says. "It has helped me and helped my daughters. When I decided to get a divorce after trying to make my marriage work for nine long years, I summoned the courage to talk about how I really felt. I took private time, wrote down my feelings, and spoke them aloud before I felt sure of what I wanted to say to my husband. It wasn't easy. His reaction wasn't what I would call calm and collected, but I was proud of myself for taking control of my situation and myself.

"In a strange way it's like the time I learned to ride my blue Polar Bear bike," she remembers. "When I started, the training wheels were on, and I thought they were 'stupid.' I just wanted to get going! So the training wheels came off and my mother taught me to really ride. She kept encouraging me, saying, 'You can do it. I know you can.' She stayed with me. It wasn't like she gave me a push and said, 'Good luck. You're on your own.' She was there, she was supportive, and she was honest.

> *Success is never found. Failure is never fatal.*
> *Courage is the only thing.*
>
> – Sir Winston Churchill, British Prime Minister

"Now, when I'm in circumstances that demand straight talk, I tell myself the same thing. And you know what? It works! Recently, one of my children divorced and was complaining about not getting enough support from her ex-husband. I told her that she was responsible for her own life. Complaining is like falling in a hole and staying there. It wasn't easy to say and it wasn't easy for my daughter to hear, but I felt better for being honest. And I know that, ultimately, she respected me for being so up-front with her. She knows being honest with her means that I honestly love her."

### BARBARA

Barbara, a teacher, discovered a similar lesson about using straight talk. "Without realizing it, I was repeating a pattern from my childhood. Using straight talk changed it," she says. "Back then, I had to assume a lot of the housekeeping and cooking responsibilities because Dad was ill and Mom had to work. Recently, I had an epiphany that I didn't have to shoulder all the work in our house alone. I asked my husband to help, and he was glad to pitch in. Many times the answer is 'yes,' but you don't know if you don't ask.

"As a child, I remember feeling resentment when my brother was outside riding his bike while I was doing chores. Now I wonder: What would have happened if I had asked him to teach me to ride, or help out with the chores? Maybe I wouldn't have been fifteen before I finally ventured far from the house on my bike."

## Straight Talk: It's for Every Occasion

I was privileged to give a toast at our daughter Wendy's wedding. I felt it was one of the most important speeches I had ever presented (besides the one I gave at our son's wedding!). A few weeks later, Wendy asked me if I knew how long the toast had taken. I said I thought it was five minutes. When I reviewed the wedding video, I was shocked. It was fifteen minutes long! My daughter wanted to tell me about this because she had a feeling I was not aware of the length of my speech. I'm glad that she did because I have become more sensitive to situations and other people's timing since she brought this incident to my attention.

You might think that it was inappropriate for my daughter to be so candid. No, I'm pleased that she was because I now know that she understands how to use straight talk. If she can use it with her mother, I know she uses it with others. Her approach was very positive and very sensitive. She took the risk of telling me her feelings because she hoped I would find the information useful. Today we laugh about it whenever we go to weddings and listen to long-winded speech-givers.

Let's face it: Change won't happen if a person isn't aware that his or her behavior is causing a dilemma. That's why it's important to go to the source of a problem instead of complaining to others.

*"I THOUGHT THIS WOULD BE A GOOD TIME TO ASK WHEN I GET MY NEW SCHWINN — "*

## Be Direct and Truthful

Straight talk is a true act of communication. When should you speak up? As soon as you reasonably can. If you wait too long, you may forget what you needed to say, which can leave a nasty residue of resentment that can explode at the wrong time or at the wrong person.

The more you tell the truth, the more you begin to trust yourself to speak the truth at appropriate times. When you let go of your negative feelings, resentments are released and you stop blaming others.

It's hard to know when to speak up, but it's equally difficult to know when to let something drop. To gain perspective, try to imagine how important this incident will be in six months. If you think it will still be important, it is best to say something now. If it would sound a little silly in six months, let it drop immediately.

The first few times you offer up straight talk, you may feel overwhelmed with anger and resentment. Make sure you don't fall into the cynic's trap and say, "It's not going to do me any good to say anything anyway."

Do not use straight talk while you're still feeling strong anger. First, count to twenty. Close your eyes and breathe deeply. Write down what you want to say. Maybe even wait a day. Do whatever it takes to get yourself under control and ready. Remember: Telling the truth isn't a license to dump your negative feelings on others.

If you feel it will help, visualize the conversation and rehearse both what you will say and the responses you imagine you will get. This will help you remain poised. Visualize an ending that will be satisfactory both to you and the person you are communicating with.

If you have a cooperative friend, you can practice the mirror exercise. As you speak, your friend will act as your reflection, repeating everything you say as well as your tone of voice and mannerisms. You may be surprised at this graphic reenactment of your mannerisms. It may be quite different from what you think you project to others.

Make a short list of major points and expected answers. Consider the other person's feelings. Begin with positive statements but be sure to get to the point. Describe the person's actions in terms of behavior, not personality. Use language that makes an impact but decreases defensiveness. Most importantly, listen to what you both are saying as well as to the tone of voice you both are using. Be aware of your own body as you watch the other person's body language. For example, does the person look at you directly or roll his eyes? Are his arms folded defensively across his chest or resting on the arms of the chair? Is he nodding in agreement as you speak or turning away from you?

Make sure the person understands what you are saying by asking him or her appropriate clarification questions. For instance you can ask, "Are you with me on this?"

Not everyone will like you or your style. You won't please everyone. That doesn't mean you have to automatically accept other people's negativity. If someone presents his or her anger, you don't have to accept it. You can evaluate the honesty and motives and decide to reject the outburst. This reduces stress, builds your self-confidence, and boosts your self-respect. It also tells the world you are an honest person.

### MAURO

Mauro, the captain of a cruise ship, makes straight talk a top priority with his crew, his family, and when called for, with his passengers, too. "There is no other choice for me. What you call straight talk is basically being honest and up front about what is going on. Foremost for me, it's about communication. I expect my crew, for example, to be as truthful with me as I am with them. This builds a solid foundation of trust that is imperative no matter where you are, on sea or on land.

"It was the same way when I rode my bicycle all over Europe. My father was transferred a lot, and that experience took us to wonderful places. He taught me to ride in Italy and I still remember the thump of the bike as I rode over the old, gray stones on a panoramic road. My father stressed safety and preparation in increments, which wasn't surprising because he was a mechanic on a ship. With me, he took one training wheel off at a time. This really helped me appreciate the importance of taking only the necessary risks in life.

"Nowadays, when my ship is out on the ocean, I have the same sense of confidence I did back then on my bike in the streets, knowing that clear communication is the force that allows clear sailing."

## The Basic Tenets of Straight Talk

1. By standing up for your rights, you respect yourself and gain respect from others.

2. Sacrificing your rights usually results in training other people to mistreat you.

3. If you don't tell others how their behavior negatively affects you, you are denying them an opportunity to change their behavior.

4. You can decide what is important to you. You don't have to suffer from the tyranny of "should" and "should not."

5. When you do what you think is right, you feel better about yourself and experience more authentic and satisfying relationships.

6. There is much to be gained from being able to stand up for yourself and respecting the rights of others.

7. When you use straight talk correctly, everyone involved benefits.

## The Implications of Straight Talk

If you adopt a straight-talk communication style, keep the following questions in mind:

1. What do I gain by not using straight talk?

    ✦ Protection from others?

    ✦ Praise for conforming to others' expectations?

    ✦ Maintenance of a familiar behavior pattern?

    ✦ Avoidance of possible conflict or rejection?

2. Would I be willing to give up any of the above? Which ones?

3. What do I lose by not using straight talk?

    ✦ Independence?

    ✦ The power to make decisions?

    ✦ Honesty in human relations?

    ✦ Others' respect for my rights and wishes?

4. Do the gains of using straight talk outweigh the losses? If so, why? If not, am I willing to make the change? Can I enlist the support, understanding, and cooperation of others involved, either in the situation or in my life?

## Choose Straight Talk Words Carefully

Use "I" statements rather than "you" statements:

*"I would like to tell my stories first without any interruptions, then I'd like to hear yours," versus "You always interrupt my stories."*

Use factual descriptions instead of judgments or exaggerations:

*"I will be required to place you on two days' probation without pay if you continue to arrive after 8:00 a.m.," versus "If you don't change your attitude, you're going to be in real trouble."*

Express thoughts, feelings, and opinions reflecting ownership:

*"I think tabling this question would allow us time to gather more data," versus "Don't you think we should table this for now?"*

## Gear-Shifting Action Steps

1.  Identify whether the person you want to talk to is indirect or direct. Indirect people don't like confrontation, so start speaking at a slower pace. Direct people like to hear results, so conversations with them need to be fast-paced and to the point. Write down the straight talk conversation you want to have with this person.

    Describe this individual's personality.
    How do you think he or she will react?
    What do you want to say?

2.  Listen creatively.

    What could the worst reaction be?
    Your response might be: _____

3.  Set your goal.

    What changes in behavior do you want to see?
    What does the other person want?
    Your expectation is: _____

4. Negotiate to a win-win solution.

    List specific examples of behavior you would like to see change.

5. Create closure.

    You agreed to _____

    The other person agreed to _____

    (Shake hands)

6. Evaluate the process.

    You will meet to evaluate on_____ (date).

## Exercise: Steps Toward Conflict Resolution

1. Identify the situation.

    Person: _____

    Conflict: _____

2. Make an appointment to discuss the conflict.

    When: _____

    Where: _____

    What will you say to arrange this appointment? Try, for example, "I need to talk to you about our working relationship."

3. Put forward the "I" message.

    I feel (your responsibility) _____

    when I (non-judgmental)_____

    because (how it affects you)_____

Example #1: *"I feel* frustrated *when I* plan brainstorming sessions to improve morale *because* no one gives suggestions at the meeting."

As opposed to: "People complain and whine about morale before the meeting yet they don't contribute."

Example #2: *"I feel* frustrated *when I* repeatedly ask for help *because* no one listens to me. I work like the rest of this family and need input from everyone."

As opposed to: "You are a bunch of lazy bums and you never help me out. I'm sick of the couch potatoes in this family."

## The Tactful Message Exercise

*T = Tell.*

Tell the other person how you view his or her unwanted behavior. Describe what he or she has been doing.

*A = Affect.*

Describe how this behavior affects you, the relationship, or the organization. Use "I" statements and express *your* feelings about the behavior.

*C = Change.*

Request a specific change in the other person's behavior.

*T = Tradeoff.*

State what the other person may gain by changing his or her behavior. You can also point out what he or she may lose if your attempts to point out the rewards of the change are not successful.

# chapter 6

# Enjoy the Moment

## "Experience the Sheer Joy of the Wind in Your Face"

### Find Your Joy, Moment by Moment

Joy can be measured by how much you are able to live in the present moment. So much precious time is wasted worrying about the future. Do you spend a lot of energy obsessing about matters that haven't happened yet? Are you constantly living in the future, worrying about attaining goals or dreams that lie ahead? If so, the present is flying by so fast, you aren't living in it.

Most people I meet tell me that worrying cripples their lives. In response, I suggest that they try to think positive thoughts when this happens. This sounds so basic, yet I know that it is not easy to do.

Years ago, I used to waste a lot of time before a keynote speech by worrying about the program. I would think, "What will happen if I bomb? What will happen if the meeting professional isn't pleased? What will happen if the audience walks out?"

Today, I quiet my mind before each presentation. I've also added twenty minutes of upper body stretches as part of my daily routine. This additional preparation really melts the tension from my neck and shoulders. I'm ready for the world, even if the day doesn't unfold as I had hoped it would. I prepare myself as well as possible for roadblocks that come my way, including rejection, cynics, traffic jams, and computer problems.

Recently, I bought a new computer, and the salesperson promised me all the support services that I requested. When the technician called to get directions to my home, I reviewed the promised services with him. The technician informed me that he couldn't perform all of the promised requests. I called the salesperson, who then told me to buy a competitor's machine, since he was too busy to deal with the problem.

I could have yelled (and who would have blamed me) and wasted a lot of energy. Instead, I calmly called the computer company, spoke to someone in customer service, and explained the situation. The next day a technician arrived at my doorstep, and was able to deliver the promised computer services. Guess what? I wasn't charged for the eight-hour service visit.

Why waste precious time worrying and getting stressed out? This one incident, where I kept my cool and stayed focused on the moment, brought me such joy! I received a new computer, all the support I requested, and even better customer service than I had counted on.

"LOOK WHAT I GOT! A SCHWINN!"

> *It always seems to me that so few people live. They just seem to exist, and I don't see any reason why we shouldn't live always until we die physically. Why do we do it all in our teens and twenties?*
>
> – Georgia O'Keeffe, painter

To quiet your negative inner voice, try to override counter-productive thoughts so that they don't overtake you. Simply "turn off" the destructive thoughts. It's like switching channels when you realize that you're not enjoying a television program. It may take some mental training before it becomes a habit, but switching "mind channels" will soon become a natural part of your thinking process.

You can also do little things to help you stay clear and present. I've found that listening to waves from a sound machine relaxes me as I fall asleep. The sounds transport me mentally to a beach where the sun warms my skin as the seagulls fly overhead. As an added benefit, the waves also help block the sounds of noisy neighbors!

Keep telling yourself that success is the only option. When you do this you'll watch the worry begin to drop away and real joy take hold in your life.

## "What's in a Bike?" — More Stories of Triumph

### RON

Ron, an attorney, credits his success to the positive attitude of his parents. "From the time my dad taught me how my bike when I was six, I learned the value of positive thinking," he relates. "That really helped me appreciate everything around me. I'll always remember the sheer joy of riding my dream bike, a Super Goose equipped with sturdy handlebars, grips, and heavy pedals. The bike was the means to explore trails, or get 'lost' with my friends on back roads. Today I

> *I got to thinking one day about all those women on the Titanic who had passed up dessert at dinner that fateful night in an effort to "cut back." From then on I've tried to be a little more flexible.*
>
> – Erma Bombeck, humorist

get the same rush from scuba diving, skiing, or flying a plane. When people react negatively to my choices, I sense their fear of trying new things but I don't let it stop me. I feel that if it brings me enjoyment and I am as careful as I can be, why not do it?

"Now, with my own children, I encourage them to tap into their free spirits. After all, it is important to enjoy and respect the value of living life to the fullest."

### JESSICA

Jessica, a minister, finds joy in lots of things. "I suppose some people might think these things are ordinary," she says, "but isn't that the point? Finding joy in the simple things is the way to live a full life."

Growing up in a rural setting, Jessica remembers hard-working parents and a devoted grandmother. "Every spring, when the lilacs bloom, the scent reminds me of the cologne my grandmother dabbed on her lace hanky. I spent a lot of time with her—when I wasn't doting on Tootie, my pet bunny, who I used to put in my bike basket and take on rides. I didn't get to spend much free time with my parents because they were so busy. They didn't have the time to read to me or take my brother and me to the movies. It wasn't until I was grown that I realized work is love made visible. They demonstrated their feelings to my brother and me by giving us a peaceful, clean home.

"With my own children, I've found joy in spending time with them and letting the house get a little messy. It's a personal choice that we all have to make: Find what makes you happy and do it."

## Give Yourself the Time You Need

Running all day can make you miss so much. I hear so many people complain that they don't know how to enjoy their lives anymore. Sleeping, reading, playing with their kids or grandkids, riding their bikes—there never seems to be enough time. I surveyed 1,000 adults and a whopping 40 percent reported that they would prefer to spend vacation time at home.

Making time for yourself is not a luxury; it is a necessity. In the scheme of things, our time here on earth is so short. If we don't make some changes, how many of us, as we take our last breath, will truly be able to say, "I feel satisfied with who I was, and with what I did. Life was an adventure." When people are on their deathbeds, they don't say, "I wish I had put more time in at the job."

**JERRY**

Jerry, an attorney, knows how to balance his life so that there's always time for joy. "I'm so aware of working smart and playing hard," he says. "I learned how to enjoy life for a simple reason: my childhood didn't have a lot of pleasure in it. First of all, there was no privacy. Between me, two brothers, two sisters, my parents, and both sets of grandparents in one house, we were always in one another's way. And getting a bike? That was really tough, because my parents wouldn't permit it after one of my sisters had an accident and broke her permanent teeth. I taught myself to ride on a borrowed bicycle. Every time I wanted to practice I had to trade a toy for a ride.

"There were some spectacular moments. We spent hot summer days playing in the water when the fire hydrant was open. Twice I won a jackpot on television—out of 100,000 contestants! I won two bicycles as prizes. It was unbelievable!

"I decided early on to support my kids when they wanted to learn and take risks. I believe that undertaking new challenges is the road to enjoyment. I also feel that we, as individuals, are responsible for our own successes and failures. To me, that is part of the joy of discovery—and of life."

**MOSS**

For Moss, a cruise ship tour director, delight can be found everywhere. "When I was growing up in South Africa, our house was always filled with friends and family. My mother, who had a wonderful sense of humor, loved company. Watching her enjoyment gave me a clear vision of how my own life should be," he says.

"When my daughter taught herself to ride a bike I was so proud. I thought, 'like father, like daughter.' It gave me such pride to see some of my traits in her, just like I have some of my mother's traits. This connection is a source of such happiness for me; I think about it often, especially during difficult times. And it always gives me courage."

Ask yourself these questions to determine if you are living your life to its fullest:

Am I living as the person I want to be?
What have I really been doing with my life?
Am I fulfilled?
What brings me joy?
What do I need to let go of to be fulfilled?

## Discover Joy Right Where You Are

While making a living is part of the arc of a successful life, living successfully completes the circle. Make it your goal to enjoy life as much as you can. Living life with a passion gives others the unique gifts only you possess.

> *All my possessions for a moment in time.*
> – Queen Elizabeth I on her deathbed in 1603

> *There are only two ways to live your life. One is as though nothing is a miracle. The other is as though everything is a miracle.*
>
> — Albert Einstein, physicist

Remember: While striving for more success can give you many luxuries, there are few accomplishments as rewarding as being content with what you have.

To help make this happen, concentrate on what is in front of you when you walk or ride a bike. Slow down, see the trees, smell the flowers, hear the birds. Enjoy what is right in front of you when you are at home, too. Do your best to turn off your challenges from work. Pay attention to family members. Listen to conversations at home, especially during meals. Do what you can to make sure the precious time you and your loved ones share is as pleasant as possible. Fulfillment comes when you realize what really matters.

## LUANNE

Luanne, an employee relations manager, credits her mother as her inspiration for finding joy everywhere. "She was like a big kid, always looking for ways to have fun," she recalls. "Even though we didn't have much money, my mom saved up for a used two-wheeler bike. She sanded it down, painted it, and presented it to us at Christmas time. All winter it sat in the basement. My sisters, brother, and I took turns sitting on it. We couldn't wait for the weather to get warm so that we could go outside and ride it for real. When it was time to learn to ride, she steadied us until we were ready to go out on our own. And that gave her a lot of joy, too.

"When I ride a bike now I often think of my mother and how she watched out for all of us. I also think of my bike time as private time. I know that it's okay to venture out on my own."

## SABRINA

Sabrina, an equal employment specialist, had a similar experience. "My first big bicycle was a sparkly blue Schwinn with white hand-grips and a silver banana seat. I loved looking at the seat as much as riding on it; just sitting on it made me so happy! My parents were a big part of the experience. They felt parents and children should do everything together, so they were there when I first learned to ride. My parents encouraged me, saying, 'You're coordinated, you can do it!' I was only five, but I rode around as my parents watched with pride. It was a wonderful day. I guess it's no surprise that I believe being full of enthusiasm is one of the best cushions a person can have against the 'bumps' that inevitably come along."

## Gear-Shifting Action Steps

Read the directions before doing this exercise.

1. Close your eyes and count to ten. Inhale. Exhale. Think of a relaxing place. How does this feel? What do you hear? Why is this place so special? Stay there for a few moments. Do this exercise during times of stress. This mini-vacation can help you focus.

2. List activities you want to do. They could include taking a trip, going for a daily walk, or organizing your day.

   Now take a look at things on the list you want to do in the future and prioritize them. To accomplish them, you must start out with a sense of purpose.

> *We are always getting ready to live, but never living.*
>
> – Ralph Waldo Emerson, writer

3. Appreciate what you have instead of concentrating on what you want.

   Try to eliminate these kinds of thoughts: "If I had more money, I'd be more relaxed," and "When I was younger, I was happier."

   Try substituting, "I am continually changing and evolving into a more fulfilled person."

4. Make a list of things in your life that bring you happiness.

5. What does someone else have that you wish you had? Is he or she really more fulfilled than you are? What do you have that this person doesn't have? It's always easy to look and see that the grass is greener. How about taking a closer look at your own backyard?

6. Which moments have been your most satisfying and most treasured? Create a mental photo album of these experiences that you can turn to as a reminder to stay rooted in joy.

> ***Life itself is the proper binge.***
> – Julia Child, food expert

# chapter 7

# Balance

## "I Feel Like I'm Stuck in High Gear!"

### How to Slow Down and Stay Balanced When the Road is Bumpy

### Finding Your Balance: It's Not Just for Bike Riding Anymore

I am a true overachiever at work and at home. During the holidays, when someone asks me to bake cookies, I don't bake two kinds, I bake six. I just love to put 100 percent into whatever I do. My kitchen looks like I enjoy it—every baking utensil is well-used!

Overachievers have a passion for what they do. They also pay a price for that passionate single-mindedness. My son, Ron, always says, "Mom, you never have a problem getting on the treadmill of life. You just don't know how to get off." He is so right! I am constantly working on changing this aspect of my life. This is not a little ironic, since I work at helping others find balance in their own lives. I know I'm not alone in this, because many people tell me that they can advise friends about trying to find balance while struggling to achieve equilibrium themselves.

What about you? Do you put lots of energy into your projects? If you do, make sure you enjoy the experience. Take the time to stop and look at your accomplishments. This will help you gain the balance you want in your life.

## "What's in a Bike?" — More Stories of Triumph

**KENNETH**

Kenneth, an attorney, knows how to balance his life. "I learned an important lesson early in my life. For one thing, my father had to spend a lot of time away from home for work. It seemed to me, as well as my siblings, that this wasn't right—for him, our mother, or for us. Now that I'm a parent, I make sure I spend a lot of time with my family," he declares.

"The other 'balance' lesson involved my bike. I never had training wheels. I just got on the bike, even though my feet hardly touched the pedals, and my father gave me a push. It took a few times for me to find my balance, but I soon had it. Finding that balance has steadied me to this day. I know that as long as I keep trying, I'll achieve success."

**ANDRE**

Growing up in suburban Moscow, Andre, the only child of engineers, was taught to ride his bike by friends. Now a naturopathic doctor, he recalls that riding the bike was a matter of learning to balance and moving forward. This theme has played out in his life over and over again.

Andre started out in engineering, but later followed his passion and became a doctor, specializing in alternative treatments. Working in a research institute, he finally had the opportunity to travel overseas to America on expeditions. This paved the way for him to leave Russia. After making preparations, he brought his family to the United States with him. His decision to leave Russia permanently was difficult. It was hard to face the fact that he had no future he could depend on. His life was out of balance.

Today, as Andre reflects on his long-term goals, he says, "It is good to change courses and interests and change our paths. We don't know our capabilities. There is so much to learn and experience," he says. "There is never complete balance, only continual adjustments. But it's that movement that ultimately keeps you balanced. Overcoming difficulties in Russia, making a new life for myself in America, studying, making new friends—all these 'movements' keep me balanced."

## Lack of Balance Can Lead to Burnout

A workshop participant once asked me, "How thin can I spread myself before I'm no longer here?" She was feeling so burned out that she didn't know what to do. Continually giving to her family, her job, and her community, she needed a release to restore her balance.

The desperation in her eyes expressed her yearning for help. She began to cry when I suggested she make an appointment with herself for fifteen minutes each day. That quarter hour could be used to figure out how to delegate some tasks or just say "no" to others.

A few months later, she called me to say that she had made progress. For instance, when she was on "hold" on the phone she would do work she had put aside for those very occasions. She also understood that gaining control meant not doing everything herself. Best of all, she told me that laughter was coming more easily for her.

My "success journey" had become such a habit that I didn't know there was another way I could live. I spent so much time redoing my speeches that I lost many hours of family and personal time. A funny thing happened on the way to the top:

> *I don't think you can be a success if your business is thriving but your children hate you. I don't think you're successful if you're climbing the corporate ladder while running your health into the ground. Without this balance, we cannot achieve true success.*
>
> – Peter Lowe, management specialist

> **The most common regret of the terminally ill is:**
> **I made a living, but I never really lived.**
>
> – Elizabeth Kubler-Ross, psychologist

My programs are better now that I have chosen to take the time to smell the roses. What a relief to realize I don't need to obsess over preparation as I did in the past!

Perfecting my craft is still a huge part of my life. I have learned that spending more time with family and taking time for myself—and my bike—are also part of the ride. Solitude is no longer a luxury—it is a necessity.

Burnout isn't always bad. It's exciting to feel passionate about something. I'd rather experience mega stress a few times in my life than be bored and uninspired. Unfortunately, many stressed-out people are of little value to themselves or to others. They use their "condition" as an excuse for not doing a good job.

Sometimes, burnout may be a signal for change, an indication that major adjustments are due — especially when you spend many hours on projects and exclude your family. It is important to identify the contributing factors. By doing so you can begin to cope, take steps to change, and refresh yourself.

## Signs of Burnout

If you are experiencing these signs of stress you may be burned out and ready for a change.

1. Are you just as tired when you wake up as you were when you went to bed?

2. Do minor problems seem major?

3. Do the small pleasures of life fail to satisfy you?

4. Is your productivity waning?

There are times you need to be out of balance in order to get where you want to go. For instance, if you decide to earn a degree or receive a promotion, you will pay a temporary price in your personal life. Discuss this conflict with the people closest to you and help them see how your personal growth is worth the sacrifice of balance for a few months.

## Find What is Missing: The Value Connection

The quickest way to identify what is missing in your life is to know your core values. Recently, a workshop participant shared that he felt overcome by stress. He traveled often in his job and he missed being with his son. After he took a core value exercise, he realized how important family was to him. I'm happy to say that he made a major job change. He is now making more money and doesn't need to travel.

Values are the qualities that have tremendous impact on your life. Core values are the laser beams that keep you focused on achieving fulfillment.

There are many different values. Here are just a few that are important.

*Empathy:* Helping others.
*Knowledge:* Discovery; love of learning, books, and workshops.
*Commitment:* Ideals, strong convictions for a cause.
*Power:* Praise, honors, titles.
*Aesthetics:* Beautiful scenes from nature, architecture, or art.
*Independence:* Uniqueness, empowerment, creativity.
*Personal:* Peace, comfort within ourselves.
*Wealth:* Security with money.

**ANDREA**

Andrea, a systems analyst, knows what has value to her. "When I was growing up, my folks focused on achievement. It was a lesson that stayed with me. Unfortunately, when I grew up and went to work, I let my job take over my life. My marriage suffered, and my whole life was out of whack. I had to get some control back, so I sought therapy, which really helped. While talking to the therapist, I remembered my grandfather teaching me how to ride a bicycle. It was the first time I had felt completely self-sufficient, the first time I knew I could rely on myself to get something done. The therapist helped me see that there is more than one way to achieve balance and get things done.

"Now, when I'm at work I give my company all I've got," she says. "And when I'm home, I'm completely focused on my family, especially our son. I go into another mode and embrace my personal life as much as I do my professional life. It didn't happen overnight, and I had to work at it—but it's so worth it. I take the initiative and rely on myself to get something done."

## Time: The Great Balancer

Can you guess what one of the biggest motivators of today's workers is? The answer is, control over their time. All of us have twenty-four hours in a day: no more, no less. It's how we use this time that really counts.

What is holding you back from making a change that would give you more time for yourself? Can you say "no" to the things that are not consistent with your core values? To be fulfilled, sometimes you have to say "no." It takes courage to define your

*Realistic living is the courage to stay sane in a crazy world. The sun requires no courage to rise in the morning, to shine in the day, to "die" in the evening. But we—the living, breathing, passionate people— we do.*

– Sherwin T. Wine, Founder of the Center for New Thinking

boundaries and maintain authenticity. Ask yourself if you spend your time on things that really matter to you, or if you spend time on other people's goals.

It takes discipline to achieve balance. Many people are not aware that they don't have to be workaholics. Workaholics do have an enormous amount of discipline; they're just not applying it in the best way. They need to learn to keep work at work.

## Balance Your Waking—and Sleeping—Hours

We all know about the importance of exercise, proper diet, and relaxation. However, there is another basic need most of us don't get enough of—sleep. So often people say how tired they are. Having the self-discipline to make a realistic bedtime for yourself is essential. With enough sleep, you will deal better with stress.

A couple of months ago, I was traveling to a workshop. The airport was closed due to weather conditions (does this sound familiar?) and I had to sleep in the airport, because all the hotels were booked. I finally flew out the next morning after only two hours of sleep.

The workshop lasted five hours, but somehow the adrenaline kicked in and everything worked out. I couldn't figure out how in the world I was able to pull this off. Then I remembered that the day before the flight, I had gotten a good night's rest. If I had had two or three days of sleep deprivation, the workshop would certainly not have worked out as well.

## Learning Balance, the Joyce Way

Remember my own bike story in the Introduction, where I learned the value of practice? It only took me 45 years to learn the second part of my father's message because I hadn't been ready to hear it!

The second part was "trust yourself." We already have what we need to succeed if we believe in ourselves. Every time you

> *The meaning of life comes from the realistic hope*
> *that there is enough satisfaction around to balance*
> *out the painful frustrations of human existence.*
> *The real world cannot promise you a rose garden.*
> *But there are lots of flowers along the way.*
>
> – Sherwin T. Wine, founder of the Center for New Thinking

accomplish something, you take risks along the way. Each success expands your confidence level so that the next new risk or fear won't seem so big or intimidating. This trust comes with experience and with age.

It also took me a while to learn to trust myself, even during slumps. I finally discovered that sometimes our disasters turn into opportunities. When you trust yourself, things eventually work out. Believing in yourself is a great comfort and confidence-builder, since life throws us so many challenges. When you believe in yourself, you begin to look at life head-on and say, "I will meet this challenge, just watch me!"

How about you? Are you *living* your life or just earning a living? It's your choice. Just remember, practice makes perfect, and trust is a big part of the formula, too. Enjoy the journey and take the ride of your life as often as you can! You'll be amazed at how soon you will find *your* "balance."

### JOHN

John, an Air Force captain who grew up in Asia, received his first lessons in balance as a child. "My sisters and I shared one bike, which was difficult, because we all wanted to ride it all the time! It was a sweet little bike, with a white banana seat and a hand bell which we chimed nonstop. Our dad was our training wheel. He taught us how to ride and instilled his lesson on balance in our lives: Don't strive for excess, whether it is for money or fame or anything else. Lead a balanced life—that is what will bring you happiness.

"Now, as an adult I know he was right," John says. "I teach my son the same lessons, both on and off his bike."

## Gear-Shifting Action Steps

1. Try this to address what parts of your life aren't working for you. Call a buddy and share your thoughts. Ask this person what he or she would like to change in his or her own life. Call or e-mail each other once a week, month, or whatever is comfortable, to check on your progress.

   Remember: This is not a guilt-measuring exercise but one to help you grow and discover what you can do to be more fulfilled. If you "slip" backwards, don't berate yourself. Instead, promise yourself to do something every day to help achieve your goal.

2. Write down three activities you wish you had more time to pursue. Next to each one, write down how much time each week you want to spend at this activity. Be bold. This is your life! Set aside time to nurture yourself every day. It is so important to be alone and have time to reflect or simply enjoy the quiet. Alone time can include practicing yoga, spending time in nature, or just taking a relaxing bath. Do you set aside some time for yourself every day? Think how doing so would add peace to your life.

3. What is your favorite time of the day? How do you use this time?

4. Think about your favorite activities and list at least ten things you enjoy doing. Are there both activities with people and solitary activities? How often do you spend your time doing these activities?

5. Draw a circle and divide it into six pieces, like a pie. Label each piece of the pie with the following words: work, family, friends, play, quiet time, sleep. Now think about how you can build more quiet time into your life. For instance, you can get up a little earlier to read the paper or reflect on the day ahead. These few minutes are a gift to yourself, so be sure to schedule quiet time for yourself every day until it becomes a habit.

## Core Value Exercise

Mark your top ten core values on the first line; then prioritize them on the second line.

   ___  ___   1. Financial security

   ___  ___   2. Respect from others

   ___  ___   3. Recognition: being well-known

   ___  ___   4. Personal freedom and independence

   ___  ___   5. Family structure and cohesiveness

   ___  ___   6. Spirituality

   ___  ___   7. Punctuality for self

   ___  ___   8. Efficient use of time

   ___  ___   9. Personal solitude

   ___  ___   10. Power over others

| | | |
|---|---|---|
| ___ | ___ | 11. Personal creativity |
| ___ | ___ | 12. Being appreciated |
| ___ | ___ | 13. Enjoying good health |
| ___ | ___ | 14. Taking on challenges |
| ___ | ___ | 15. Experiencing excitement and adventure |
| ___ | ___ | 16. Competing |
| ___ | ___ | 17. Being productive |
| ___ | ___ | 18. Feeling inner peace |
| ___ | ___ | 19. Experiencing love and affection |
| ___ | ___ | 20. Being of service to others |
| ___ | ___ | 21. Interacting with others |
| ___ | ___ | 22. Gaining wisdom and insight |
| ___ | ___ | 23. Enjoying cultural activities |
| ___ | ___ | 24. Having intimate (truly honest and close) relationships with others |

Now list your top five core values. These are your ultimate internal motivators.

Finally, ask yourself how often your personal and professional life matches your core values. What could you do to remedy any discrepancies?

# chapter 8

# Professional & Personal Growth

## "You Can Teach an Old Biker New Tricks"

### Never Stop Learning!

**Growing Requires Asking Questions**

Leonardo da Vinci had an insatiable curiosity about life and an unrelenting quest for learning. He wouldn't take "yes" for an answer. Da Vinci dissected each part of the human body from different angles and even studied his own illness as he lay dying. He said, "The knowledge of all things is possible. I shall continue and never tire of being useful. The desire to know is natural to good men."

Have you ever watched an eagle fly? It does not fly straight across the sky but around the same area over and over again. Each time it flies from a higher vantage point to gather more information.

In order to learn about where we are, or what we need to with our lives, we must explore the possibilities. Only by doing so will we find out who we really are.

> *If you always do what you have always done, you will always get what you have always gotten.*
>
> – Anonymous

## "What's in a Bike?" — More Stories of Triumph

**STACI**

Staci, a product designer for a glassware company, sees a direct link between learning to ride a bike and her growing artistic ability. "My first bike was kind of decrepit, with dented training wheels, but there was a kind of nobility to it," she recalls. "My father wanted to teach me, but he didn't get to it soon enough. One day I sat down and studied my friend riding his bike. Then I told him I wanted to try it. I learned instantly.

"When I got my next bike, which was pink and sleek, I saw it as my chariot. I even won a race in it, just like in *Ben-Hur*," she laughs. "It was a fundraiser for the American Cancer Society Bike-a-thon. I was given a trophy for riding sixteen miles, the longest distance for kids under seven years old.

"Winning that race gave me permission to seek other goals, and see what I could accomplish. That race ultimately led me to Asia, where I studied design. The temples, shrines, and gardens were so beautiful, so peaceful. I felt an incredible serenity that moved me to design jewelry. Then I received an award for a brooch I created for an international competition. And once again I grew, not because I had won but because I kept seeking and growing."

*Centuries ago a Chinese general wrote:*
If the world is to be brought to order,
  my nation must first be changed.
If my nation is to be changed,
  my hometown must be made over.
If my hometown is to be reordered,
  my family must first be set right.
If my family is to be regenerated,
  I, myself, must first be.

*" IT'S BEEN YEARS SINCE I'VE BEEN ON A BIKE."*

## Growth in the Workplace: It's Not a Contradiction in Terms

Here is a sampling of complaints I've heard from management and non-management alike. Some employees are disgusted with their co-workers. They feel the work ethic is going down the tubes. These employees want to enjoy their workday; they like their jobs. The challenge for them is figuring out how to deal with mediocre co-workers.

Sometimes senior employees believe they are "entitled," meaning different standards apply to them because of their years of service. This attitude causes friction among newer employees.

In response, I tell my audiences that what has worked in the past won't necessarily work today. In today's marketplace there are new work realities. The fact is, there are no guarantees anymore. All employees need to be realistic about what their companies "owe" them.

At the same time, the expression, "It's not in my job description," is a weak response in our present economy. Giving more—

not less—to an employer is more important than ever because it shows how valuable you are—that you indeed have a lot to offer and are willing to make the commitment to do so.

Whether you're one of the rare people who has worked at the same company for twenty years, or have been recently hired, a commitment to improving yourself and showing your desire for professional and personal growth will strengthen your position. Consider it a gift to yourself to invest in your own career growth and develop new skills.

There's no question that change is constant. New bosses, job descriptions, offices—they're all part of the modern employment "package." That's why one of the keys to being successful is to anticipate change. Accept the past and look forward to the future. This includes considering what is coming, what needs to happen, and how you can rise to the occasion. Remain flexible and instead of changing *with* the times, try changing just a little *ahead* of them.

### IVAN

Ivan, a guide in Mexico, recognized his skills early in life, although he had to ride over more than a few bumps before he could apply them. "I was always interested in the scenery," he says, "so it makes sense that my work evolved from what I liked." Never knowing his father, Ivan was fortunate to have a devoted uncle who taught him English, as well as how to ride a bike. "Learning English was a real growth experience for me, because it prepared me for the future," he remembers. "Now I take American tourists around my country, and show them the land I'm proud of. I can speak to them and understand their questions.

"As a little boy, riding my bike, I only spoke Spanish. My uncle gave me a dream of being more, understanding more. Now I give my children the same lessons."

> ## *I knew that I would be going places and I just wanted to know where I was when I got there.*
>
> – Michael Jordan, basketball legend (when asked why he majored in geography at the University of North Carolina)

Management guru Tom Peters said, "Only those who constantly redo themselves stand a close chance of staying employed in the years ahead."

We all have blind spots, so ask people you trust to make suggestions about areas in which you could use some growth. They will probably give you some insights about yourself you weren't aware of. This may feel like a risky exercise, yet it's a very helpful one.

I always ask my audiences to fill out evaluations on how I can improve. This feedback helps me grow, although some of the suggestions have been hard for me to accept. At the beginning of my career, people liked my programs, yet thought they were missing an element of fun. As a result, I started studying how to add more humor. I might have missed learning this important skill, which has now become a wonderful part of both my work and home life. I like to think of constructive feedback both as a seed for growth and a gift of encouragement.

When working with companies, I ask non-management what improvements they would make if any of them were the CEO. The answers are always interesting. Here are a few of them:

+ "Make people more accountable. Employees never get in trouble and everyone knows our boss doesn't take charge. I would explain the company's vision to everyone and hold people more accountable to that vision."

✦ "I would have a meeting with a delegate from each department. That way we could figure out what was working well and what needed to be changed."

✦ "I would ask everyone to put his or her name in a hat. Every week I would grab a name from that hat and take that person out to lunch. That way I'd get to know people on a personal level. They wouldn't feel like just a 'number.' "

When I give the results to the CEOs, they see their own blind spots right away.

Morale is a subject that comes up over and over again. Management is not solely responsible for morale. You also need to figure out how to recharge your own batteries. Take suggestions to your team about how you think the group can improve morale at work. Job sharing, for example, allows each team member to understand the roles and responsibilities of fellow employees. Live plants, pictures, soothing music, and food can all make a difference, too. What additions or changes in your workplace would help your team?

Remember: you want to be a fixer, not a finger pointer. It's harder to be a part of the solution if you are still part of the problem.

The goal is to fix the problem and figure out how not to make the same mistake again. This may sound basic, yet blaming others is a real downer and waste of good energy at work or home. If others are playing the blame game, do what you can to stop it. Ask for a "time out!" and an explanation. You can try saying: "This is not going to help solve the problem, so let's move on to the solution." It is amazing how positively people react to this kind of suggestion.

## MICHAEL

Michael, a writer, used a variation of this approach to help solve a specific problem. When his former business partner took all his money, Michael and his wife turned adversity into opportunity. "We didn't throw up our hands and say, 'We're sunk now.' Instead, we focused on hard work and other sources of income. We didn't lose control of our family, our friends, or ourselves. In a way, it reminded me of learning to ride a bike. My mother was hanging laundry in the backyard and I kept pestering her. She told me to go ride my bicycle, and I did, even though I hadn't been able to do it before. Today, whenever a problem strikes—big or small—I confront it. And you know what? The problem gets solved."

Finally, adding positive values to your organization will help you grow, too. Attend networking meetings and share what you have learned with your team about how to make your company stronger. You never know who you will meet at these events. Many companies reward their employees who find quality new-hires for the company. This is an extra benefit, since you are also finding people who will bring professionalism to your team. In this way, you're taking direct control of your own future.

## LIZA

Value is a concept that Liza, who works in sales and marketing, understands well. "I've always tried to do whatever I'm doing the best I can. This way, I value what I am doing and give worth to the projects I'm working on. Perfectionism was always my standard, and I owe it to my older sister for showing me this. Of course, she learned to ride a bike first.

"I, too, used this perfectionism to learn how to ride my bike by myself. It was an elegant navy two-wheeler with chrome trim. I was very independent. I kept practicing over and over again until I did it.

Our driveway had a slope. I think it actually helped me learn a little quicker.

"My parents always stressed work before play. I try to temper my perfectionism. I still cook all our meals and keep the house spotless in addition to working part-time. I'm working on relaxing more with my family. We are having a lot more fun."

Continued growth is each individual's responsibility. But people often ask me, "Joyce, why should I do my personal best? The company or the boss will make more money, but I'll still get the same paycheck." Doing your best does make your department stronger, but it goes way beyond that.

The good news is, if you continually grow you become stronger and better able to take advantage of the opportunities that will come your way. What you're doing is grooming yourself for your own best success. You never know where your rewards will come from or when. You always want to be ready to grab on to them when they come along!

## ANGELA

Angela, who co-owns a housekeeping business, understands that growing as a person is a lifetime goal. "My husband and I are teaching our children to be polite, especially to older people. I know they will meet challenges just like I did, but that's every reason to maintain the right behavior, not lose it," she says. "I left college after two years because I was married and expecting our first child. Now I'm back in school, completing my degree. It's like I felt when I climbed on my sister's bike for the first time. I said, 'I want to learn.' I feel exactly the same way now."

## JONNA

Jonna, a domestic violence counselor, strives to do her best every day. "When you ask me about a bike, I bet my story is different," she ventures, "because, to me, that red and white bike with the banana seat wasn't a symbol of freedom. I always stayed close to home, riding with my neighborhood friends. I guess I wasn't ready for any kind of independence.

"Now that I have a son, I'm trying to raise a kind and all-around sensitive person. I think the fact that I minored in women's studies makes me approach parenting a different way. I can't change the world, but I can be responsible for my choices and help my child and others follow and realize their dreams. Change is measured one event at a time. When I think back to my bicycle, I realize that I made a change when my training wheels came off. Sometimes I have to look back in order to acknowledge how much I've accomplished. Then I can move forward and grow even more."

## ANGIE

Angie, a paralegal, always attempts to do her best. "I learned to ride a red and silver bike that my mom bought from the Salvation Army. All the kids in my age group were riding two-wheelers, so I decided to learn how to ride my bike without training wheels. I took the training wheels off myself and began practicing. It wasn't easy. If I fell to the left, I would land in the street. If I fell to the right, I would land against homes with asbestos shingles. By the second day, I had learned to ride. I had the cuts and bruises to show how hard I had worked at it.

"I'm the same way as an adult. I read a lot because I want to keep growing. I persist with challenges until I get them right. If I fail trying one way, I'll attempt to succeed another way."

Personal excellence is the result of caring more than others think is wise, risking more than others think is safe, and dreaming more than others think is practical.

A few years ago, I read an essay my daughter wrote for an MBA class about the role models in her life. She selected me as one of her role models, which I count as one of the most important achievements in my life.

One thing she remembered were all the personal growth books that I read for fun on family vacations. What kinds of books can you add to your reading list for personal and professional growth? Every time I hear people interviewed about their success they say that reading is one of their passions. As a 93-year-old workshop participant once told me, "I've learned that I have a lot to learn."

## BRIAN

Brian, a doctor, spends his life learning by taking risks. "My parents were extremely conservative people who believed that honesty was crucial, and that a person was responsible for everything he did. Consequences were clear: if you did something right, then you might be rewarded. If, however, you did something wrong, then it was pretty much determined that something bad would happen. Not surprisingly, my parents weren't risk-takers," he says.

"But I'm different. I discovered that just trying something new is worth the risk. I certainly felt the same way when I first rode my bike. We lived in an apartment complex filled with alleys and bushes. There were always a lot of kids around to play with. Once I learned how to ride, I pedaled through those alleys, which were so narrow I could stick out either arm and touch a wall. I recall the coolness of the brick on my fingers, even in the summer.

"I also pedaled away from home, which was so empowering. I could go to the store by myself, see a ball game, or visit another school. What is more fun than riding a bike?

"Ever since then I have traveled through life, looking for new places, new sensations. I don't like sitting in one place too long. I think all my interests are built on what intrigued me as a child. It's as if the alley walls are still supporting me. I don't have a fear of failing because how far can I fall? And I continue to ride a bike because it's exhilarating and fun. I love the speed, taking me to new adventures."

> *We are what we repeatedly do. Excellence then, is not an act, but a habit.*
>
> – Aristotle, philosopher

## Gear-Shifting Action Steps

Continually exploring new things creates a constant journey of self-discovery. You may pursue new interests by learning about a variety of authors, movies, vacations, or even recipes. Your world will be enriched and you will discover new possibilities you didn't know existed. Even if you feel fulfilled at this moment in your life, I challenge you to find new areas of interest. Ask yourself:

1. What subjects would you like to know more about?

2. What skills would you like to acquire?

3. What credentials would you like to attain?

4. Are you the person you want to be?

5. Have you grown the way you like?

6. Do you see areas in your life you would like to change?

7. In which areas do you want to grow?

8. What do you have to do to create your future?

9. What have you really enjoyed doing the past few years?

> *Life is my college.*
>
> – Louisa May Alcott, writer

# chapter 9

# Goals & Action

## "What's Next?"

### Gear-Shifting Action Plans
### to Take the Ride of Your Life
### for the Rest of Your Life

## Take Action and Change Your Life

The most effective way to take action is to make changes. Change forces you to grow. You may not like doing this, but once you welcome it you'll be aware of endless opportunities. When this happens, look out! The achievers in this world are the resourceful people who learn to embrace change.

## "What's in a Bike?" — More Stories of Triumph

**BETSY**

Betsy, an executive director of a Chamber of Commerce, knows that change is challenging. "Since the time I learned how to ride a bicycle—my stepdad helped me—I have assessed different tasks and the skills needed to complete them on a scale of easy to hard. I first began riding a three-wheeler, which was pretty simple, unless I hit a big curve or crack in the sidewalk. Then I graduated to a two-wheeler, which was a big deal.

"I think things out before I tackle a job," she says. "That way, I have a strong 'battle plan' to follow. I slow down to determine what I want to do and how to get there. I don't 'look down.' Instead, I always look forward and work toward where I want to go. It worked for me when I rode my bike and it works for me today."

**CHERYL**

For Cheryl, a meeting professional, "Don't look back" is the action to follow. "Looking back, to me, means doing what you've always done. The day I learned to ride my bike, I was ready to try something new, something different. The warm wind flipped my ponytail and the sun danced off the chrome of the bicycle when my grandma told me, 'Don't look back, honey. Just pedal.' That was my grandma's philosophy of life, to never give up, to always move forward, to do what you have to do to make that happen.

"She had a lot of change to deal with; as a young widow she raised a son and ran a farm by herself. She also taught school and rented out rooms to boarders. She gave me an incredible example to follow. I tell my son that no matter what successes I've achieved in the past or will accomplish in the future, my greatest one is being his mom. I'm making sure he knows his life is going to be full of changes. I will always be there to support him through the example I set."

## Action is the Road to Success

**MONTE**

For Monte, a fine art photographer, the paths to achievement have taken many twists and turns. "Overcoming challenges defines my life," he says. "When I was a youngster I had a terrible stutter. Years of speech therapy gave me the ability and confidence to speak as a guest on radio and television shows.

"I left my first career when I was almost thirty because I was hardly ever with my family. Then I went into a business I didn't enjoy and knew I had to find some other kind of fulfillment. I then tried something totally new at age forty—photography. I have been earning a living, and learning a great deal about myself as well. I even teach photography so that I can pass on what I know. I learn from my students. I believe the basic lessons of life are instilled when we are children. We just have to remember them.

"When I first climbed on my bike I was scared, but I realized that without taking action, nothing would happen. The same applies throughout life: If you don't take action you'll stay where you are, and life will pass you by instead of you moving through it."

## LAURA

Laura, a state representative, has always had high expectations. Since the time she learned to ride a bike that was too big for her, she found her balance and pedaled off into an exciting life. "The world opened up to me that day and marked me as a risk-taker. I used to race down the street as fast as I could, just because achieving high speed was such a thrill.

"I've been in public life for over twenty years, a big challenge, because this work requires a lot of courage, both professionally and personally. I find it very exciting. It's not unlike getting on that unwieldy bike and controlling it. In fact, I still ride a bike today—only this one is the right size!"

## TIM

For Tim, a manufacturer's rep who maneuvers around the obstacles life flings in his path, moving forward a little at a time is the way to go. "When I was growing up, we were pretty comfortable. I

> *The secret of getting ahead is getting started. The secret of getting started is breaking your complex, overwhelming tasks into small, manageable tasks, and then starting on the first one.*
>
> – Mark Twain, author

had numerous bikes. They gave me a lot of mobility—I could just get on and go.

"Later, when I grew up and got divorced, my entire life changed. I felt as if I was on a symbolic bike that was taking me to new places where I had to adapt. I moved to a new city where I didn't know anyone. I had to start over completely," he remembers. "I was paying child support and lived in one-room apartments until I was promoted at work and could afford a bigger place. I'm still mobile, even if the steps I'm taking now are small ones, one after the other."

I believe that no matter what your background is, if you want something badly enough and work hard enough for it, you can succeed. In order to achieve your goals you need to make them a "have to have it, can't live without it" proposition. There will be times when you may need to modify what you are doing to get what you want. There will be times when changes happen that you didn't expect. It's often hard to adapt to these changes, because routines are comfortable and familiar. Even simple adjustments can be difficult.

During my presentations, I use different techniques to help people understand their reaction to change so that they can learn to adapt to it. I often ask people to take off their watches and put them on the other wrist until I finish my speech. The reaction is amazing. Participants find it awkward to look at watches on the opposite wrist. Even changing seats in order to meet new people makes them uncomfortable.

I use the following exercise in my "Full Speed Ahead: Become Driven by Change" program. I ask participants to select a partner. Then I direct them to stare at each other for two minutes without talking. Some people laugh. Others turn beet red from embarrassment. I have found a great many people feel uncomfortable because they are doing something new and rather intimate.

When the two minutes are up I have them turn their backs

and change three things about their appearance. They usually remove ties, shoes, glasses, etc. Sometimes I ask them to remove three more items. I can always tell by their body language if they are uncomfortable with so much immediate change.

Interestingly enough, no one ever "borrows" an item from another person in the room, despite the fact that I never tell them *not* to do this. When I point this out, the audience realizes that they could have borrowed a pen, glasses, or some other item from someone else around them. After they change three things, the other person is supposed to guess what it is they have changed. The minute the exercise is over, participants claim their belongings and put them on. As soon as they can, when the pressure is off, they return to their original appearance—their comfortable ways.

One point of this exercise is that no one has to go through change alone. Surprisingly, this is a very new concept for some people. But as you've seen throughout this book, the people interviewed spoke of the support they found while learning to ride their bikes. I've discovered, through trial and error, when to do things on my own and when to ask for help. Change is a lot easier to deal with when you ask others for help.

Another goal of the exercise is to help people find options to make their lives and careers easier. Remember your first bike ride? It was exciting, scary, and empowering all at once. Remember, too, that there was probably someone there to help you. So, continue to be aware of and ask for help from the people around you. Listen to people who are enthusiastic. Ask them why they love what they do. They are not in possession of some magic formula. People who feel energized realize the excitement of looking ahead and finding options all the time. That doesn't mean they aren't aware of where they've been. Of course they are! They may glance in their rear view mirrors, but they also concentrate on the road ahead. They want to focus their energy on what life is going to offer them, not what it may take away.

## MAX

For Max, a financial advisor, learning how to accept help gracefully was part of his first bike lesson. "My brother helped me, and I never forgot it. I now realize that his being there allowed me to make a big change in my young life. Once I knew how to ride, I had a sense of freedom I had never experienced before. When I taught my daughters to ride bicycles I took the training wheels off one side at a time, so that they could learn to steady themselves. I also taught them a lesson I practice every day: Don't hesitate to help someone if you can. I strongly believe in lending a hand to assist people in business. I encourage the people I work with to seek me out when they need advice. My door is always open.

"I look at things in a positive way. Even when I experience disappointments, I try to keep looking ahead to what's possible now instead of back to what could have been. This is my philosophy and it's helped me throughout my life. Several years ago, for example, I quit my newspaper job. I felt it was time for a change, but my boss didn't want me to leave, so he gave me a six-month leave of absence, which gave me the big window of opportunity I needed.

"I applied for several brokerage jobs but didn't get any of them. After I interviewed for a particular job I really wanted, I went back to the man who interviewed me and said, 'There's no reason why you shouldn't hire me. I think you're making a big mistake.' And you know what he said to me? 'Max, because you came back and told me that I should hire you, I'm going to do it.' And that's what he did. I never forgot how this man helped me when I was ready for something new—just like my brother did when he encouraged me to ride my bicycle."

## GEORGE

For George, a sales representative, getting help was a pivotal event in his youth. "My dad was very successful. He changed careers and did incredibly well each time. The first bike he bought me was a black Schwinn English racer with red, white, and blue streamers, but he was too busy to teach me how to ride it. The superintendent of our apartment building saw me with the bike and helped me out. He kept encouraging me, saying, 'You can do it, don't worry about it! Look straight ahead so you won't fall!'

"He was right! I understood I wanted to ride and was willing to do whatever was necessary to make that happen. I never forgot the help I received that day, or the lesson I learned. Maybe my father didn't teach me how to ride, but he gave me the means to do it. Maybe the superintendent taught me because he felt sorry for me. Neither of these things matters, because I saw that help is always out there, right in front of you. You just have to 'see' it. If you want to do something badly enough, you can do it. Just get the help you need to make it happen. I think we're all masters of our own destinies."

## MIKE

Mike, a housing director, has had setbacks, yet they never stop him. "I just look for another opportunity," he says. "My parents taught my brothers and sisters a fundamental lesson we've never forgotten. We understand life isn't handed to us on a silver platter, and we have to work hard to get what we want. Our dad showed us this when he taught us how to ride our bikes. He told us he would support us, but we had to practice to find our balance. Once we did, we gained a new independence. It was true then and it's still true today. There are no straight paths, and the road of life is full of detours. Still, I believe I can get where I want to go. All I do is keep trying."

## VICTORIA

Victoria, a business owner, gained similar insight. "I was five when my father taught me to ride my first bicycle, which was a Huffy. He kept saying, 'When you fall you must get back on the bike. Only by falling can you find your balance.' The words stuck with me and I still apply them today. 'Go for it' is my motto.

"Being persistent is important. I keep trying because I've learned there is more than one way to do and see things. This mindset helped me get through my parents' divorce, which was tough. During this time my stepfather adopted me. I know the man who taught me how to ride a bike was my 'real' dad because he was there for me."

*People are always blaming their circumstances for what they are. I don't believe in circumstances. The people who get on in this world are the people who get up and look for the circumstances they want; if they can't find them, they make them.*

– George Bernard Shaw, playwright

Fascinatingly enough, there is one person who never learned how to ride a bike, but his perspective and life lessons apply to everyone.

### SHERWIN

As a boy, Sherwin, now a rabbi, found he enjoyed walking through cities because he learned more about people that way. "Watching men, women, boys, and girls taught me how they responded to their environment. The way they crossed the street, or whether they were smiling or frowning spoke volumes."

His outlook is candid: "Don't try to change the past and don't make excuses for behavior. Go ahead and do what you want to do."

As far as bicycle lessons go, he says, "Whether you ride a bike or not, you have to pick yourself up after disappointments. Failure is an important part of life because it challenges you to find confidence in yourself. You must tell yourself that you are not going to get what you want unless you dust yourself off and try again. You certainly don't want others to think you can't follow through. Facing any challenge, and overcoming it, leads to self-esteem."

Thank you to Marilyn Rowens, poet, author, and cartoonist, for giving me permission to use her poem, *Our Children*. This poem expresses the kinds of questions and observations we all must ask ourselves in order to continue taking the ride of our life, for the rest of our lives. It expresses a parent's wish for her children—the wish we often have for ourselves.

### OUR CHILDREN
### by Marilyn Rowens

I look out of the window and I see my son riding his tricycle
My daughter is digging in the sandbox.
What kind of person do I want my child to be?
I want my child to be understanding, patient, intelligent,
Caring, generous, loyal, kind, reasonable, ethical, courageous,
Friendly, honest, good-humored, open.
Perfect?
I must teach him that he doesn't have to be perfect.
I must teach them both to solve their own problems.
As much as I would like to absolve them of pain,
They must face their pain and survive it.
I cannot do it for them.
Yet, it is my responsibility to help them become strong
And I am not perfect
I can only do my best.
So I want for them more than is possible for them to have.
I want them to feel no pain.
I want them to have no struggle.
I want them to feel no rejection.
But in this real world, that is fantasy,
And I must teach them reality.

> *You miss 100% of the shots you don't take.*
>
> – Wayne Gretsky, hockey superstar

## Gear-Shifting Action Steps

1.  Babies learn by imitating their mothers and fathers. As
    adults, role models can guide and inspire you toward
    realizing your potential. That's why it is important to
    choose wisely about who and what to imitate.

    Find others who are living the kind of life you want.
    Answer the following questions to help you discover
    what you need to add or eliminate from your life to
    achieve your goals and live your dreams.

    a.  What is working in your life?

    b.  What do you need to change?

    c.  What is one thing you can do to enhance your life?

2.  The following steps have been taken from numerous
    programs I've given on making successful changes.
    They really work!

    a.  Decide which current belief or behavior you want
        to change.

    b.  Use role models to accelerate the pace. Ask them
        how they achieve their goals.

    c.  Understand that you will do far more to avoid pain
        than to gain pleasure. (Going on a diet is painful
        and eating sweets is pleasurable.)

    d.  Link pain to your current belief to move away
        from it. (Eating candy drains energy.)

    e.  What is the cost if you do not change? Concentrate
        on how not changing your belief will be more painful
        than changing it. (Candy can put weight on you.)

f.  Concentrate on how changing your belief will bring immediate pleasure. Identify a new empowering belief. (Eating an apple, instead of candy, will give you energy.)

g.  Become aware of routines that you have created. What habitual behaviors have you developed? (The TV goes on and you head for the kitchen to get a snack.)

h.  Knowing does not change your old beliefs. Doing does. Take immediate action.

3.  Develop an action plan for successful change:

a.  Identify the change you want to make.

b.  What are three simple action steps you can take immediately?

1. _____

2. _____

3. _____

c.  What is the pain you have associated with in the past? (e.g., feeling low energy due to weight gain)

d.  What are the benefits (pleasure) you will gain by taking action? (e.g., feeling better)

e.  Write down new routines that you will create with the new change.

---

*The best way to predict the future is to create it.*

**– Peter Drucker, management consultant**

f.  Write down what it will cost you not to achieve the goal. Link pain with not achieving that goal.

g.  List five reasons why you must change now.

1. _____

2. _____

3. _____

4. _____

5. _____

h.  Write down all you will gain from achieving your goal. Link pleasure to achieving this goal.

## Create Your Own Bike Story!

These are the questions I asked during the bike interviews. Take some time to answer them and you will create your own bike story. Please feel free to send me your story. If I use it in a speech or another book, I will send you a gift. Have fun with this!

1.  Who taught you how to ride your first two-wheeler bike?

2.  What lessons did you learn from your parents?

3.  What is the impact of those lessons on who you are today?

4.  What values are important to you?

5.  What messages have you taught your kids or other children that are in your life?

6.  What challenges were you able to turn around so that they became opportunities?

7. What was a turning point for you in your life?

8. Do you have any regrets?

9. What is preventing you from living a more fulfilled life?

10. What makes you laugh?

11. When was a time you felt really alive?

12. What do you feel passionate about?

13. What has your career path been like?

14. How does your bike story represent who you are today?

# Conclusion

I am honored that you took the time to read this book. Thank you for investing part of your life with me.

As you've just read, constant improvement and practice are both part of life's journey. Look at what you have already achieved! Savoring these moments is an important part of your ride.

While you are the master of your own bike, you cannot control a lot of things, like the weather, traffic, or bumps in the road. Life allows some easy coasting, other times you must travel over rocky roads. No matter which obstacles you confront, it is up to you to decide where you want to go and how to get there.

Your life is in front of you, so put on your helmet, shift gears, . . . and *TAKE THE RIDE OF YOUR LIFE!*

# Bibliography

Bach, Richard. *Jonathon Livingston Seagull*. New York: Avon Books, 1970.

Cathcart, Jim. *The Acorn Principle*. New York: St. Martin's Press, 1998.

Frankl, Victor. *Man's Search for Meaning*. New York: Washington Square Press, 1985.

Gelb, Michael. *How to Think Like Leonardo Da Vinci*. New York: Delacorte Press, 1998

Gesell, Izzy. *Playing Along*. Minnesota: Whole Person Associates, 1997.

Harari, Oren, Ph.D. *Leapfrogging the Competition*. California: Prima, 1959.

Raspberry, Sally and Padi Selwyn. *Living Your Life Out Loud*. New York: Pocket Books, 1995.

Rowens, Marilyn. *2000 ... And Holding*. Michigan: Mini Lecture Press, 2000.

Senge, Peter. *The Fifth Discipline*. New York: Doubleday, 1990.

Sinetar, Marsha. *Do What You Love, the Money Will Follow*. New York: Dell, 1987.

Weiss, Joyce. *Full Speed Ahead*. Michigan: Bloomfield Press, 1996.

Wine, Sherwin T. *Staying Sane in a Crazy World*. Michigan: The Center for New Thinking, 1995.

Joyce Weiss, The Corporate Energizer®, is an internationally recognized expert on creating a more energized life—on and off the job. Part of her expertise is helping people find and maintain a balance between their personal and professional lives so that they can bring their absolute best to both.

As a speaker, she takes the time to understand the unique pressures and challenges her clients face. She then customizes her programs to meet these needs in a way that helps audiences identify simple solutions they can begin using immediately. Some of her most popular programs available for customization are *Full Speed Ahead* and *Take the Ride of Your Life!* (also the titles of her two books), as well as *The Power of Straight Talk,* and *Yes, There is a Second Right Answer.* Joyce's powerful, proven techniques have helped thousands of individuals renew, reenergize, and reclaim their passion and productivity.

Joyce is a Certified Speaking Professional (CSP), the highest certification a speaker can earn from the National Speakers Association (NSA). Only seven percent of the association's 4,000 members have achieved this high honor. Her corporate clients include AT&T, Ford Motor Company, Blue Cross/Blue Shield, Allstate Insurance, and the American Banker's Association. Government agencies include the Internal Revenue Service, the U.S. Department of Defense, and American Red Cross.

*You may contact Joyce Weiss at:*
*Phone:* (800) 713-1926
*E-mail:* joyce@joyceweiss.com
*Visit her web site:* www.JOYCEWEISS.com

# Joyce Weiss
## The Corporate Energizer®

## Speaking Topics

*Reenergize Yourself: Take the Ride of Your Life!*
Learn to take the pressures of a demanding day and turn them into exciting new opportunities. This program offers valuable insights that help audiences create more rewarding personal lives and careers by turning roadblocks into successful profits and productivity.

*Full Speed Ahead: Become Driven By Change*
Learn how to respond to change while gaining control. Seeing opportunities in change is a key ingredient in this program.

*Creating Your Own A-Team*
Learn how to excel through cooperation and increase team morale. Consensus-building and creative brainstorming are two energizing components of this vital program.

---

*Choose from a variety of customized presentations:*
*Keynotes ✦ Workshops*
*Group and individual coaching*

*Creativity: Yes! There is a Second Right Answer*
Providing opportunities for creative work will not only harvest new ideas, but will make motivation soar and job turnover drop dramatically. Participants practice exercises that make barrier-free thinking a natural behavior at work and in life.

*The Power of Straight Talk*
Participants in this program learn the skill of straight talk—speaking up when it's necessary to do so—to develop more productive relationships and reduce workplace stress.

## Other Topics

*Celebrating Diversity in the Workplace*
*Dealing with Difficult People and Situations*
*Leadership Excellence: Are Your Managers Effective or Defective?*

---

*For more information on how we can*
*help meet your specific needs, e-mail us:*
*joyce@joyceweiss.com*

# Joyce Weiss's other books and workshops

*Joyce has so many great ideas for not only dealing with change—but creating it! What used to seem like monumental challenges now seem like challenging adventures. It's amazing what happens when someone helps you change the way you see things.*

– Curt Major, President,
Harry Major Machine & Tool Company

*We're quickly seeing how rediscovering your personal passion for life directly translates into dramatic improvements in productivity on the job. Thank you, Joyce, for showing us how to keep finding more of our own greatest potential.*

– Marie Anderson, Training Director,
Wisconsin Bankers Association

*Wow! This is first-rate material from a world-class author and speaker. What's so inspiring about Joyce is that all of her advice is so useful and easy to put into practice!*

– Tom Cieszynski, Executive Director, Southeastern
Michigan Health Association (SEMHA)

*Over the years Joyce has consistently helped us to see the possibilities before us and really grab hold and take advantage of them. She has a rare talent for truly motivating others.*

– Karen Blohm, Product Research & Development,
ProNational Insurance Company

*The great thing about Joyce's books and workshops is that they not only apply to all areas of your life, but actually help you create a balanced whole out of the many parts and pieces of your life. An incredible gift.*

– Terri Moore, Director of Human
Resources, Melody Farms

*Listening to Joyce Weiss is an enlightening experience. She's smart, bright, articulate, and so full of ideas that the room just seems to vibrate with the pure energy of it all. I've never felt such a lasting impact as I have from Joyce's workshops.*

– Kim Biggs, East Coast Regional Sales
Manager, Mont Blanc Corporate Gifts

*I have nothing but the greatest admiration for the way Joyce's ideas instantly help you see the possibilities in every situation. I've been a big fan of hers for years.*

– Frank Vander Meer, Customer
Service Manager, Spartan Stores

*Joyce is one of those people you just can't get enough of. She always presents ideas in a way that makes such perfect sense. We look forward to having her at our convention year after year.*

– Heather Mathews, Meetings and Education
Coordinator, American Bus Association

*Joyce offers common-sense strategies for getting the most from yourself and your life. Listener response is always great! She's a dream guest for any radio show.*

– Marie Osborne, News Anchor/Reporter, WJR Radio, Detroit

# Hear Joyce live!

For information on having Joyce speak to your
business or organization, call (800) 713-1926

## Order Online!

You may order all Joyce Weiss books, CDs,
audio tapes, articles, and other motivational
products and gifts directly at:

**www.JOYCEWEISS.com**

# To Order More Copies of This Book

❏ Please send me ___ copies of *Take the Ride of Your Life!* for $12.95 each.

❏ Please send me ___ copies of the *Take the Ride of Your Life* original theme song on CD for only $6.95 each.

In the U.S., please add $4 for shipping and handling of the first book or CD and $2 for each additional book or CD.

Michigan residents, please add 6% sales tax.

Name _____

Company _____

Address _____

City _____ State _____ Zip _____

Phone _____

E-mail _____

❏ A check for $_____ is enclosed, payable to Bloomfield Press.

Please bill my:  ❏ MasterCard  ❏ Visa  ❏ American Express

Card number _____ Exp. _____

Name on card _____

Please mail this order form to:
Bloomfield Press ✦ P.O. Box 250163
West Bloomfield, MI 48325-0163
FAX: 248-682-0358